MW01518157

From the Stars to the Street

Engaged Wisdom for a Brokenhearted World

NOVALIS

© 2007 Novalis, Saint Paul University, Ottawa, Canada

Cover design and Layout: Audrey Wells

Business Offices:
Novalis Publishing Inc.
10 Lower Spadina Avenue, Suite 400
Toronto, Ontario, Canada
M5V 2Z2

Novalis Publishing Inc.
4475 Frontenac Street
Montréal, Québec, Canada
H2H 2S2

Phone: 1-800-387-7164
Fax: 1-800-204-4140
E-mail: books@novalis.ca
www.novalis.ca

Library and Archives Canada Cataloguing in Publication

Conlon, James
    From the stars to the street : engaged wisdom for a brokenhearted world / James Conlon.

ISBN-13: 978-2-89507-828-9
ISBN-10: 2-89507-828-9

    1. Human ecology–Religious aspects–Christianity. 2. Cosmology. I. Title.

BT695.5.C64 2006   261.8'8   C2006-905523-8

Printed in Canada.

We acknowledge the financial support of the Government of Canada through the Book Publishing Industry Development Program (BPIDP) for our publishing activities.

5   4   3   2   1   10   09   08   07

Dedication

**To all peoples and the planet,
who in their beauty and wisdom
are each a walking star,
I dedicate these pages.**

The engaged wisdom that we seek shimmers in the night sky and is transacted in the street.

It arouses the heart of the artist, brings compassion to the politician, and generates moral outrage in the mystic.

The engaged wisdom illuminates the stars and brings radiance to the streets.

As each story unfolds, we experience a new beginning, a genesis, that finds its origin in the universe and its manifestation in the revelations of our faith.

With prophetic courage we leave behind another time; we become exodus people as we heed the call to set all the captives free.

Through story and action, intimacy and contemplation, we join our energies with the powers of the universe as we embrace that great compassionate curve, the universe's arc of justice.

It is here that we realize the kingdom, the reign of God, and let heaven happen now.

Acknowledgments

To all who connect the wisdom of the far reaches of the universe with the depths of their own heart and make connections to heal our broken world, to my friends, colleagues and mentors whose vision and practice have contributed to these pages.

In particular, I am grateful to those who have worked with me on the project, including Joan LaFlamme, Erleen Palmer, Karl Zols, Marilyn Goddard, Jane Heckathorn, Valerie Bowman, John Bowman, Jennifer Sacramento and Christine Steady Ndiage, and to the people at Novalis, including Michael O'Hearn, Kevin Burns, Anne Louise Mahoney and Lauretta Santarossa.

Contents

Foreword

Each great turn of history introduces a new paradigm. This means that new forms of perceiving and interpreting reality emerge, that we are obliged to redefine the fundamental concepts that orient our social and personal lives including our concepts of God, human beings, history, the meaning of existence, and the universe. New challenges appear that demand new responses.

In this book Jim Conlon demonstrates the personal transformations and the new sense that he found in his life upon breaking through to a new vision of the universe in evolution – a vision of the cosmic energies and the interconnectedness of everything with everything else.

Jim traces his personal path from being a student of chemistry – and afterwards of theology – in university, to his interest in social sciences and communications therapy, to being a community organizer and educator. In the measure that he entered more deeply into these fields, he realized that he lacked a vital synthesis that could unite them all.

Restless, he continued searching. Everything changed when, almost in the form of a conversion, he discovered the new cosmology and the new vision of reality that flowed out of this. The possibility of a grand synthesis opened up, adapted to the new biological phase of the earth and of humanity. In this, he found new answers to the challenging problems that the earth and humanity are facing.

Evidently, this existential revolution called him to redefine the great concepts of the Christian tradition, beginning with God as a benevolent and compassionate presence that pervades all and each cell of our being, the Holy Trinity as a supreme interplay of the energies of love and communion, the human being as the moment in which the universe emerges into consciousness and responsibility – and also other concepts such as biblical revelation, grace, and sin as an expression of brokenness of heart. But the most fundamental change was to discover the wordless wisdom that is found in all the phases and in all the entities of the universe.

With intelligence and ability, Jim Conlon discovered how to articulate this cosmic revelation – the first book that God wrote – with the revelation of the Christian scriptures. Without artifice, he combines the Christian paschal mystery with the mystery of the universe, with its moments of destruction and of creativity demonstrating that chaos is never chaotic, but rather always generative of new and higher forms of complexity and of life.

This new vision helps us to understand the fact that we are coming to the end of a planetary era, as has occurred so many times in the past. We come to a critical juncture, as Jim affirms, that obliges us to make fundamental changes. We have devastated ecosystems, polluted the air, contaminated the soil, dirtied the waters and, due to the voracity of the industrial process, each year we have caused hundreds of species of living beings to disappear forever.

Instead of simply lamenting this situation, Jim Conlon accepts the challenge to activate those universal energies that can save us. This is what he calls *geo-justice*: to do justice to the earth and to all its beings. His first book carries this significant title: *Geo-justice: A Preferential Option of the Earth*.

This geo-justice is born of what he calls *engaged cosmology*. This means the capacity to contextualize and connect all phenomena in the perspective of the universe. All is permeated by the energies that burst forth in the first moment of the big bang, from the stars to the street, as he expresses so well in the title of this book. Everything is related with everything else and nothing exists outside this relationality. Each person is bound up in this immense network of energies and is an actor in the evolutionary process.

If we are at the end of a biological era, this signifies not an absolute catastrophe but rather an opportunity for new energies and possibilities to spring forth from the quantum vacuum – that is, from the original fountain from which all beings emerge. A new era can begin, and we can help with our consciousness, our action, and our social and ecological justice to inaugurate a new horizon of meaning and hope.

From the Stars to the Street is a call to hope in the midst of the dramas we are living in these days. The energies that permit us to sustain this vision are derived from the wisdom of the universe, the wisdom of religious traditions, and the wisdom of the Christian paschal mystery. Jim envisages a time when the earth will resurge with integrity, beauty, compassion, care for all life, and a deep sense of sister- and brotherhood among all human beings and with our brothers and sisters in the biotic community.

Jim's book inspires enthusiasm, trust, and hope – indispensable virtues for those who want to heal and save the earth and humanity.

Leonardo Boff
Theologian and Member of the Earth Charter Commission

Introduction

For years, Jim Conlon, director of the Sophia Center's Wisdom School at Holy Names University in Oakland, California, has been working to articulate the inclusive vision that inspires him and inspires the Sophia Center's program.

In his new book, *From the Stars to the Street: Engaged Wisdom in a Brokenhearted World*, Conlon takes another major step toward elucidating that vision. For Conlon this vision is the culmination of his life journey and the integration of all the different stages of that journey into one vast yet concretely engaged whole.

He reflects on his journey from a small town in Canada to his college and seminary training, to his work in the parish, then to his turn to community organizing in the Saul Alinsky tradition, followed by a turn to personal and group therapy, then to popular education in the tradition of Paulo Freire, and then to his discovery of the new universe story through Thomas Berry and others. In this book he seeks a recapitulation and synthesis of this whole journey.

After work in the parish as a young priest Conlon realized the profound systemic injustices of the social system and the need for structural transformation through empowering the community itself to control its own destiny. Immersing himself in the community-organizing program of Saul Alinsky in Chicago, Conlon dedicated some years to this work of social justice through empowering the oppressed people themselves. But eventually he began to see the limitations of life poured out in changing systems at the expense of the inner life. He saw marriages torn apart and lives burned out by those who gave their all to changing unjust structures without attention to their own inner nurture.

Turning to an innovative program in the Toronto area, communication therapy, Conlon devoted himself to the inner nurture and personal growth that had been sorely neglected in his seminary education, pastoral work, and dedication to community organizing. He learned how to tell his own story and confront his limitations, including the ways in which anger at social injustices can hide deeper conflicts within the self. This was a vital stage to find a new balance and harmony within himself.

But also he gradually realized the limitations of the turn inward – the problems of trying to heal the inner self without reference to social evil and injustices. He began to seek a new integration of inner healing and healing of society.

The reductionism of the psychoanalytic tradition tended to portray the divine as a projection and left the larger spirit that sought union with God repressed. Traditional psychotherapy too easily dismissed social action as an excuse for unresolved personal conflicts.

Paulo Freire's work in popular education became a vital tool that brought together personal conscientization and social transformation – an interactive process of healing the self and liberating society. For Freire, learning to tell your own story, liberating yourself from the silences imposed on you by the oppressive system, was vital to gaining literacy, liberating the ability to speak, to interpret, and hence to change the larger world.

The last missing piece for Conlon was the discovery of the new universe story, interpreted through the new vision of cosmology begun in Teilhard de Chardin, and developed in the thought of "geologian" Thomas Berry. Here all the other pieces of the puzzle began to fall into place, to fit into the larger context of the unfolding of the universe itself. The wounded and fragmented self and the violence and injustice of the larger society found their context in a humanity deeply out of touch with the universe and its unfolding patterns of life. This wounded self and society could then be recognized as reaching a crisis point in which the old civilization built on dominance and exploitation was disintegrating.

At the same time, a new self and society is being born, rediscovering its deep union and communion with God, not a God far away and disconnected from our embodied selves, but a God manifest in cosmic creativity, a God embodied in the cosmos. The hope for the birth of an Ecozoic Age in which humans reintegrate the ways they live with themselves and with each other into the cosmos, into their relationship with air and water, plants and animals, can, from the Christian perspective, be seen as the promised redemption of the earth, the promise of the Kingdom Come, when God's will is done on earth, as it is in heaven.

It is this vision of integration of self and society, personal healing and social justice in a cosmological context that Conlon seeks to articulate in this inspiring book. To see both the crisis of humanity on earth in its dangerous times of terminal destructiveness, yet at the same time to see this death as itself a process of rebirth, of resurrection, into redeemed life, is the vision Conlon expresses in *From the Stars to the Street*. Here we find a combination of deep analysis and poetic excursions that seeks both to enlighten and to inspire the energy and action needed to join in the "Great Work" of this world-transforming time.

Rosemary Radford Ruether

Opening Reflections

Conceptually and metaphorically, *stars* and *streets* depict worlds apart, almost opposite ends of a continuum. The stars describe the galactic spheres with the birthing forth of elegant structure and pattern throughout the whole cosmos; the streets depict the basic stonework for human, cultural communities, the realm where we eke out our existence amid daily toil and accomplishment. The stars tell the great cosmic story; the streets, our human-based hopes and dreams.

Geo-justice and *engaged cosmology* – two of the generic notions in this book – embrace both the stars and the streets, and must do so to maintain credibility. Indeed, this finely written work, adorned with poetry and personal narrative, is entirely about the integration that requires us to keep our gaze on the stars while we daily walk the streets: "We are together on a journey from the streets to the stars, relentlessly in search of an engaged wisdom to heal a brokenhearted world."

Geo-justice, defined as a preferential option for the Earth, was the title of Jim's first book (1990). Here he weds this earth-based approach to justice-work with the contemporary challenge of *engaged cosmology*. Beyond the fragmentation which fractures our thinking and dissipates our creative energy, Jim articulates an integrated vision with *compassion, engagement and participation* as central elements.

The heart of this new vision is the readiness to embrace cosmology as our primary and fundamental context. This is the quantum leap millions have yet to make, one that becomes more urgent every day as we witness the petrified vision and devastated earth of our confused and brokenhearted world: "Engaged cosmology brings hope to a humanity wounded by a prevailing culture of dominance and oppression."

The human person must embrace the transformation of the "street"; the justice activist must organize with global vision consistently in mind (as did Saul Alinsky and Paulo Freire); religion, education, and conscientization must all contribute to the newly enlarged vision of our time: "Engaged cosmology's 'new address' is at the intersection of wisdom inscribed in the universe, tradition as recorded in Scripture, and the biographies of our lives."

Yes, the stars and the streets can meet! And the ensuing integration will bring healing and fresh hope. At the end of this inspiring read I am left with one daunting question: will we humans rise to the challenge – and will we have the wisdom to embrace it before it is too late?

Diarmuid O'Murchu, MSC

A Compass for the Journey

There are two approaches to a journey. One is to pick the end point and determine the best way – usually considered the fastest, smoothest, shortest route. The other is to keep the end point in mind, certainly, but to focus as well on the journey itself. With this second approach we take detours and slow down in order to enrich our journey. We take time to watch a hawk gliding through the sky, to delight in the texture of a leaf on a common weed, or just to enjoy the flight of a goldfinch passing our office window.

From the Stars to the Street is an example of the second approach to the journey. We wander with author Jim Conlon as he reflects on his journey, which, like our own, is travelled on a path blended from our spiritual traditions, our personal story, and the Great Story of the universe as it unfolds in our particular time and place, enhanced by our actions for a better world for ourselves and our children.

The reign of God is the end point, but Conlon's journey winds through fascinating meditative territory en route. Best of all, his reflections invite us, his readers, to slow down and savour the path on which we find ourselves and the companions – human and non-human – with whom we share it.

Joan Weber Laflamme

Preface:
Guiding Stars for the Journey

*Once the truth has made its presence felt in a single
soul, nothing can ever stop it from invading everything
and setting fire to everything.*

—*Teilhard de Chardin*

Wellsprings of Life

Uprisings emanate
within the soul of the people
each hungry for wisdom,
each longing for bread.
Uprisings are nourished
by the song of the swallow,
the whisper of the breeze,
the caress of a child,
the love of a spouse.
Uprisings emanate
from galaxies and stars
as they shimmer among us
in the corridors of life.
They stride
into the inner cities
and savour the sunshine
on the beach.

In all their hearts they sing
love letters to Earth,
each one inscribed
with the signature of God.

Our Integral Presence

*You don't know something is true until it has
changed your life.*

—*Jim Wallis*

In my own journey I have experienced many cultural waves that have altered my perspective on my place in the universe, my faith tradition, and my action in the world. My study of chemistry at Assumption University of Windsor and work in Canada's largest industrial research laboratory in Canada's chemical valley altered my world and my understanding of my place within it; the study of theology at St. Peter's Seminary before Vatican II indelibly shifted my perspective on God and the impact of Christianity on everyday life.

However, it was not until I entered Therafields, a psychotherapeutic project on communication therapy, that a new and deeper challenge for integration entered my life. As a participant in what was known as the Catholic Group, whose members had similar backgrounds to mine, I discovered that my core beliefs and understandings about life had found a new context in the therapeutic process. My early experience and knowledge of spiritual life took on an existential focus. The great dramas of experience portrayed in the paschal mystery and the courage of the prophets came home to me. It was as if I had split off from my previous formation; the therapeutic journey became the place where my values could be experienced and lived out.

As the years went by, my participation in community organization took on a similar tone. The ability to act, the desire to go within the action, and the search for a pattern of meaning became the tenets of my new commitment. As an educator, I learned that I must die to being a teacher and rise to becoming a student. Once again I found that my cultural context had become the container of my spirituality and, in some way, an arena for the discovery of my life and purpose.

More recently, my introduction into the new cosmology has accelerated this shift. The story of the universe from the fireball to the emergence of the human has presented a challenge and opportunity unprecedented in my life up until now. Suddenly, the categories that previously housed my spirituality and faith journey have become inadequate. The words of J. Phillips ring in my ear: "Your God is too small." I find amazing new insights:

- The universe as well as the Bible is scripture.
- The Trinity is communion, differentiation, and interiority as well as Father, Son, and Holy Spirit.
- Death is rebirth and return to our origins.
- Faith is trust in the unfolding process of existence rather than a matter of doctrine.
- Revelation is found in our moment-by-moment experience, not wholly contained in books on systemic theology substantiated by quotations from the Bible.
- God is a compassionate and benevolent presence who permeates every cell of our existence rather than a transcendent judge who hovers over us toting up our faults and inculcating fear.

And thus my work toward personal healing and responsibility in therapy, my work to empower the poor and the oppressed, and the adventure of critical reflection toward transformation take on a new, fresh and more spiritual perspective. The spiritual journey becomes an awe-filled and wondrous universe when "God is in all things, all things are in God." The divisions I had previously maintained between the universe, my faith tradition, and the narrative of my own journey shaped by the cultural moments of therapy, organization, education, and justice became one.

My either/or world becomes a both/and world; the work of my unfolding journey takes on a new perspective. It is as if I have stumbled upon a new language for the engaged wisdom that can heal our brokenhearted world. As I work toward becoming a more fully integrated human presence, I see the connections, and what I call an engaged cosmology comes more clearly into focus. This engaged cosmology will involve the integration and access to powers of the universe, the fresh energy that is available to us in our spiritual traditions, and the actions that become available to us and flow out of every moment of our lives.

As each of us strives and struggles to make this integration possible in our lives, together we will be collective instruments of a new era of human-earth relations. We will move toward a world unprecedented in our time: a world where we can awake each morning and know where we are; a world where we can with confidence nurture our children and promise them a better tomorrow; a world where peace is possible, health the birthright of every species, beauty the result of geo-justice-making, and engaged cosmology the musical mystery of all three.

From evolutionary science to quantum mechanics, from Freudian psychology to seeing the psyche as a context for galaxies within, from community organization to creating a space from which beauty can shine forth, we are together on a journey from the streets to the stars, in relentless search for the engaged wisdom to heal a brokenhearted world. Our commitment to continue the journey will be a function of our capacity to experience deeply the gift of inspiration and hope.

James Conlon

I had wondered what was holding the country together, what was keeping the universe from cracking in pieces and falling apart.
—*Thomas Merton*

Inspiration and Hope

Help us to be always hopeful gardeners of the spirit
Who know that without darkness
Nothing comes to birth
As without light nothing flowers.

—May Sarton

The question I ask, in this time of chaos and fragmentation, is how a spirituality of inspiration and hope will shape and focus the future. Will it offer a vision that will illuminate and encourage the vulnerable, the poor, and the brokenhearted? If someone were to ask what gives me inspiration, joy, and hope, I would answer: These are the things that give me inspiration and hope:

- An enduring belief that tomorrow can be different from today. I am convinced that despite the opaqueness of a world withering in poverty and awash with war, in a larger sense of things not now clear or understood, something good will come from the apparent devastation.

- The healing power of the beauty that I experience with the smile of a child, the delightful humour of a friend, or a gorgeous sunset over the Pacific Ocean on an autumn evening.

- Trust in a loving and benevolent God who gives me an abundance of freedom and love.

- The conviction that the incarnation continues to happen; that the Bethlehem of today is manifest in the bud of a crocus, the birth of a puppy, the gentle greeting of an elder, each bathed in the sunshine and shadows of the day.

- The struggle for justice, not the victory; the deep knowing that life is about being engaged.

- The transparent nobility of the poor and dispossessed, both human and non-human, which bring me closer to myself, to compassion, and to my God.

- The energy and vision of friends with whom I gather in classrooms and community centres and who share with me their vision, nobility, and strength.

- The privilege of knowing the lives and writings of people I admire and being touched by the magnificence of their souls.

- The conviction that my life is marked, like everyone's, with an imprint of destiny and a growing realization that all life is a gift.

- The opportunities I've had to savour beauty, experience love, embrace creation, and make a modest contribution to the Great Work of our time, which illustrate the truth of these words: "Only when it's dark enough can we see the stars."

- Memories and recollections that remind me that justice-making is a joyful and celebratory act. I recall marching down Woodward Avenue with Martin Luther King, Jr., singing "We Shall Overcome"; joining the United Farm Workers in front of a supermarket in Toronto in their march for justice; taking part with thousands of people in San Francisco to express our objection to the war in Iraq.

- The conviction that justice-making is a theatre for self discovery, a prayer, an authentic expression of the gospel, and an opportunity to let heaven happen now.

Signs of current improvement that nurture my inspiration, joy, and hope include:

- The children who will inherit the land.

- The new initiatives emerging across the land from the souls and imagination of a people. This new era of longing and desire connects to the depths of ultimate mystery.

- The eruptions of creativity manifest in radical newness, spiritually inspired moments from peoples of all cultures, traditions, and regions of the world.

- The fresh energy and zest for life that is being born from our discovery that we are genetically coded to live filled with love in a universe that fills our hearts with wonder and surprise.

- The growing realization that we live at the dawn of a new time, and that young people of all ages are taking up the banner of change.

- The electronic communication that unites the people of a barrio in Latin America to those living in a high-rise apartment in Toronto, London, or New York, where people instantly become aware of a tsunami in Indonesia and the political events of the day. Today the Global Village envisioned by media culture philosopher Marshall McLuhan has become a reality. The young of today and the young at heart have taken up the banner of justice, a banner of inspiration and joy, a banner that will make a better world for the children.

All that gives me inspiration, joy, and hope is best summed up in the words of poet Ruben Alvez:

> What is hope ... suffering and hope live from each other. Suffering without hope produces resentment and despair. Hope without suffering creates illusions, naivete, and drunkenness. Let us plant dates even though those who plant them will never eat them.... We must live by the love of what we will never see. Disciplined love is what has given prophets, revolutionaries, and saints the courage to die for the future they envisioned.

In my heart I believe that the joy, inspiration, and hope I experience will be authentic and true when I participate fully in relieving the grief and sorrow of others, especially manifest in the poor and the poor earth so that we may share in a mutually enhancing life.

With each passing day a growing number of people ask how they can make a commitment to life, to communion, to humour, to love, and to creativity. They want to provide assurance for a viable future for the planet and for our species. Only when people are willing to change their lives and integrate awe and wonder with strategy and action will we know that as a people *all* creatures may live.

Spurred on by the words of Isaiah, who wrote at a time when the destruction of Jerusalem was imminent, I hope for a time when "they shall beat their swords into plowshares." Only then will we experience the wonderful world expressed in a song made famous by the late Louis Armstrong: "I see skies of blue and clouds of white, the brightness of day and the darkness of night, and I think to myself, what a wonderful world."

I hope for a humanity that will emerge from this turbulent moment of confusion to heal the chasm between people and the planet.

As we look toward and anticipate the future, we direct our attention to the newborn chick; having been nourished by all that was available inside the shell, it breaks through the shell in pursuit of new nourishment and new life. The lesson of this breakthrough is that new life demands, as Teilhard reminds us, a shattering of the old. Perhaps the fracturing and brokenheartedness that we feel so keenly in today's world is a precursor to the hope and surprise that will accompany the new world already happening and coming together in our midst.

If we cling to the identities given to us by the structures of the current paradigm, we are going to perish as a people and a planet.

> Listen deeply and from silence see each moment as revolutionary.
> Respond courageously to the challenges of our time.
> Discover a deeper destiny and radiating presence.

The future of humanity lies in the hands of those who are strong enough to provide coming generations with reasons for living and hope.
—*Vatican Council II*

An Invitation

We live in the network of cosmic influences as we live in the human crowd or among the myriad of stars.

—*Teilhard de Chardin*

These pages are an invitation to embark on a journey marked by your connection to the cosmos, your faith tradition, and your personal story.

For more than four decades, I have been participating in such a journey. Now, at this stage of my life, I have begun to explore how these three aspects (cosmos, faith, personal story) have shaped my life. Together, we will embark on a process of integration.

First, my personal story: As the youngest child of Irish and French Canadian parents, I grew up in a small village in southwestern Ontario – Canada's most populous province – that borders Michigan in the United States of America. This was my "terrain of consciousness." My story is one of economic depression, the joy of family, and the beauty of rivers, trees and farms, each a classroom for life's important gifts and lessons. It is the story of an academic journey that began in a two-room schoolhouse and progressed to the study of chemistry at the university, theology in the seminary, social science, and eventually cosmology and spirituality. My life has been formed by a commitment to continuous learning.

I was born into and raised in a Catholic family with parents devoted to their faith. My faith tradition has indelibly imprinted and focused my journey. From an occasional catechism class as a child with no experience of Catholic schools to attendance at a Catholic university and later the seminary, with subsequent work in theological schools and graduate programs in spirituality, questions of faith and its implications for justice have been a primary focus of my adult life. Although I was always fascinated and nourished by the beauty of the earth, my introduction to creation spirituality and the story of the universe have profoundly altered my life. Now, I feel an invitation to integrate my story, my faith, and the story of the universe. These pages reflect this "work in progress."

They tell my personal story and also my desire to provide a framework for others as together we strive to locate our lives within these turbulent years at the beginning of the twenty-first century. I am attempting to bring to consciousness the engaged wisdom of the universe, which communicates the Great Story with sight and sound, colour and fragrance, beauty and breeze. This primary revelation empowers our actions and nurtures our capacity to hope. Deeper healing happens to restore our wounded Earth. Beauty envelops us as solidarity unites the pre-existing commitment of our faith with the genetic energy of God.

The most radical political act is a change of heart.

—Jack Kornfield

Teilhard often wrote of them as two stars dividing our allegiance (God and the world) ... the Divine Milieu is an attempt to show how these two stars come into conjunction.

—Thomas King, SJ

1

Beauty Shines Forth

Our call is to integrate all of this,
that is to say cosmology and the call to justice.

—*Community Action Network, Dublin*

Our lives are about a relentless search for change: an urgency to transform structures and oppression. Established patterns of injustice hold us back yet we strive to transcend desperation and transform whatever curtails our freedom and represses our ability to act. In the face of opposition, we turn inward, determined to continue the struggle. As we examine our wounds and the structures that bind us, we realize that we must radically change society and ourselves.

Strengthened by our awareness of the universe, we are energized by the cosmic context of our journey. With new confidence we visualize a planet and a people once again made whole. Toxicity and injustice dissolve in the membrane of a benevolent universe whose creative energies transform any tendencies to destroy or desecrate, creating instead the conditions that make it possible to recall and discover our story.

The work of engaged cosmology involves integration; it will be marked by moving away from any tendency to separate our secular experience and our faith tradition. Through awareness of the universe as primary revelation, we will see that God's action in the world is mediated by everyday experience. All encounters with creation, human and non-human, become sources of theological reflection. In this way the universe can be understood as a sacrament, the source and context whereby we encounter and engage the divine presence in our lives.

Callings

Living the question becomes our best response, as a brokenhearted world eagerly awaits each one's healing touch. Wisdom replaces arrogance and power becomes a collective act. Trust incarnates the new name for those committed to do whatever needs to be done so that beauty can shine forth. Vocational destiny is indeed a profound mystery.

The universe and each of our lives follow a trajectory and purpose, whatever the choice or call. The future holds unknown challenges. We make the road by walking, as each new era presents its potential and possibility. Whatever our context or call, the doorway of tomorrow remains open before us. The paths we choose contain mystery, wonder and surprise with no clear criteria by which to assume or assess the outcome.

Emergence of an Engaged Cosmology

We make the road by walking.

—*Paulo Freire*

The exploration of the relationship among the universe story, tradition, and our own action autobiography and of that relationship to our personal and cultural work is intended to help us integrate these approaches and provide a vision of the divine action in the world. The universe story, the Great Story, unfolds in four chapters:

1. **The Galactic Period:** the flaring forth of the original fireball and the formation of elementary particles. Here the originating energy of the universe gives birth to a sacred impulse of self-expression. The elemental particles of hydrogen and helium are formed, and, as the cosmic incandescence accelerates, carbon, silicon, oxygen, and iron are forged. From this original fire the geological era emerged.

2. **The Earth Period:** the formation of Earth. Geological formations of rocks and crystalline structures arise that provide the structures necessary for the biological phase that brought life to come forth.

3. **The Life Period:** life on the planet begins and flourishes. Flowers bloom, birds fly, fish swim, creatures inhabit the earth. Life shines forth in many forms, and the stage is set for humanity to appear.

4. **The Human Period:** the origin of the human and the rise of consciousness and culture. Humanity emerges empowered by the psychic energy

of the cosmos and with the capacity to reflect on this wondrous cosmic event whose integral presence on Earth makes possible a vital and vibrant planetary community. Humanity becomes aligned to the creative wisdom embedded in the dynamics of the universe itself.

Connection Making

Christianity is Developmental human time, the working out of a divine presence in the human world in terms of the Kingdom of God.... Our modern story of the universe is a new sense of the universe. These two need, in some manner, to be related.

—*Thomas Berry*

While there is not a direct relationship, I propose that there is a parallel between salvation history, as revealed in the books of the Bible, and the chapters of the unfolding universe. The book of Genesis, with its creation stories, embodies myth and revelation about the divine place in the origins of life and humanity's unfolding story. Exodus and the Prophets mark a story of liberation and the work of justice that parallel in some ways the originating energy that brought about the universe. Wisdom literature speaks of the everyday beauty of God's creation, which is in some way analogous to the formation of Earth in the Great Story. The paschal mystery in the New Testament corresponds to the universe story. The mystery of the incarnation and the sacredness of all creation find profound parallels in the emergence of life that is present in the Great Story and the dynamic of creation and destruction that permeates all of life.

Road Signs on my Journey

The Christian Church that at the same time is trying to understand its mission in terms of solidarity and liberation must engage in contemplation of the mystery of God as matrix and enabler in human life and as forward movement in history.

—*Gregory Baum*

Sometimes, as I reflect on my story, in light of my Christian traditions and the Great Story of the Universe, I pause to think about the changes that have taken place over time and the events that have shaped my sense of the sacredness and influenced my life.

I grew up during the Second World War, which followed on the years of the Great Depression. I felt the impact of poverty and experienced firsthand the relationship between religion and politics, although I was far too young to understand why my father lost his patronage job when the Liberal Party of Ontario was replaced by the Progressive Conservatives. It was commonly understood at that time that if you were a Catholic, you voted Liberal. Protestants were predictably Progressive Conservative. Religion was for the most part sectarian and culturally based. The word ecumenism was yet to enter our common vocabulary. Education was viewed as preparation for the adults' ability to handle their own personal affairs. High school was optional, and university education rare.

When my sister excelled in school and received scholarships, she did in fact go on to the university. With the door to higher education open, my brother and I followed. My mother's death at this time left me with a great amount of personal uncertainty. I chose to study chemistry, my favourite subject in high school, and philosophy. After graduation from the university I enrolled in the seminary. Vatican II was convened during my seminary days. Suddenly, fresh energy seemed to invigorate the church, and progressive trends infiltrated even the seminary walls.

As I've mentioned before, in the years following my ordination I was influenced by the cultural movements of civil rights, the Vietnam War, and Vatican II. My politics began to change; my theology did so as well. I became impatient with the resistance to change that was evident in politics, religion, and society at large.

Psychotherapy provided me with a fresh sense of freedom, a new trust in my deeper knowing about the direction of my life, and increased courage to "think outside the box." When I began to work as a community organizer in Toronto, I was probably the only Catholic priest in Canada engaged in this work. Then I met Msgr. Jack Egan and participated in the Urban Training and Community Organization and joined the Catholic Committee on Urban Ministry. I was no longer alone in my newfound work.

At this point I was convinced that the future could be created by building alternative networks that retained the core values of the Christian tradition but were more flexible and responsive to the "signs of the times." (Today, I call this as an ecclesiology of the kingdom.) Looking back, I realize that I had in some ways moved away from the schoolboy in the village of Sombra, Ontario. Yet in my heart I still felt connected to the faith and values I had learned there.

I began to work at the Toronto School of Theology in the late 1970s. I brought to my preparation for ministry my years of experience in community organization and popular education. My politics had changed, and my theology had shifted from a preoccupation with orthodoxy to a focus on orthopraxis without political references. As a Christian, I would name myself as both progressive and conservative.

My experience with a group in Toronto, Catholics for Social Change, and my association with Gregory Baum encouraged me to develop a theological perspective that undergirded the work of justice. In a very real way as we reflected on our work in justice-making we were practicing liberation theology.

As the 1980s progressed, the political and theological landscapes began to become more rigid. Political leaders in Canada and the United States, along with church leaders of many denominations, became more conservative. President Reagan in the United States and Prime Minister Mulroney in Canada exemplified this trend. John Kennedy and Pierre Trudeau were no longer our leaders!

I moved to Oakland, California, and began to study creation theology and the new cosmology. I felt a new sense of energy. I had found a new arena of exploration, a place where my values could be tested. A new passion for politics and theology as I saw them began to invigorate me. I felt a growing conviction that the hope of the future would be in cultural movements infused with spiritual vision. My place would be at the centre of the issues and at the edge of the institutions.

As we moved into the 1990s and subsequently the new millennium, a new era dawned. Amid the sunshine and shadows of today, I stop to reflect. Yes, the values I learned in my village and family are still with me; yet I have also changed radically. The world is very different from the village of my childhood. We've gone from a little radio to HD television and iPods. We've gone from sectarian religious denominationalism to a vision, among some, of a post-denominational church.

And me? I've gone from Sombra to San Francisco, from the parish to the street and the classroom. I've gone from a time of certainty to a threshold moment with many more questions than answers. I've gone from handwritten letters to electronic communication.

As I reflect on these pages, what is included and the many things yet unsaid, I think again about our withering world and see my path and the path of all creation revealed by a vast universe and the depth of inner space. *From the Stars to the Street* is language for my journey as well as a way to name the journey of people moving into the new millennium. My journey has taken me from a child on the shore of the St. Clair River to the shore of the great Pacific Ocean, two bodies of water that span lifetimes and name the passage of eras and time that have brought me to the present day. All the events of our era – cosmic, cultural, and personal – are present to us now, available as a collective resource as we move into the future.

The Journey Continues

> *Humanity is being taken to a crossroad between suicide and adoration,*
> *struggling to transform disaster into a garden of opportunity,*
> *apocalypse into rebirth.*

> —*Andrew Harvey*

We take up the challenge to heal a brokenhearted world in terrible times, times when 20 per cent of the children suffer from asthma and forty thousand children die each day of starvation while innumerable people sicken due to polluted water and air. We live with jeopardy and doubt.

Our world is fractured by open markets and a globalized economy. The temples of our time are banks and multinational corporations. Our cultural priesthood is composed of scientists who hold secrets that can annihilate the world. The "new healer" is the marketplace, where retail therapy purchases and material possessions anaesthetize the restless soul hungering for the divine.

We are called to a different world. We are being encouraged by the cosmos to take on an authentic quest, to penetrate the distortions of corporate greed and the intoxication of misguided mysticism as we answer the call to come home to our deepest desire and life purpose, to come home to our God. With each step we move toward intimacy, toward justice-making. We build the kingdom here on Earth, letting this heaven happen now as the enactment of our most profound prayer. We celebrate new life, each incarnational moment that echoes to the far reaches of the world, each place where beauty shines forth. We are astonished by dreams that originate in our imagination and are the starting point of our hope.

Returning to our origins within the context of the universe and our lives, we identify more fully with the new moment that confronts us; in this process we gain increased access to love, confidence, and trust. With increased insight into our tradition, we move forward to discover new implications and creative possibilities for engaged cosmology in our actions in the world. Through engaged cosmology we identify more fully with the planetary community in which we live. In this context, leadership can be understood as an exercise in engaged cosmology and a response to the Great Work of our time.

The Great Work is nourished by the wisdom of science, women, men, indigenous peoples, and the mystical and prophetic dimension of Christianity; it is a work that will revitalize the spirit and open new possibilities for action. The Great Work of engaged cosmology will generate a new language and a new realization in our lives. It will inspire a new vision and practice of justice enriched by an operative theology of the earth.

The Challenge of the Moment

There is no scientific evidence for separation.

—David Bohm

Our challenges are unique to this moment. We need to transcend any tendency toward discouragement, uprootedness, isolation, passivity, and resignation. Engaged cosmology gives hope to humanity wounded by a culture of dominance and oppression. It provides a language and approach that allows us to give voice to and take action to transcend the problems. Through mediating structures we initiate new actions that are positive, constructive, and transformative.

Engaged cosmology comes out of imagination and courage. It is not written down in a book; it is inscribed in our lives, our spiritual journey, and the constellations of the universe. It is conceived out of struggle and the quest for fulfillment; it is energized by courage and fresh ideas. Engaged cosmology will be born out of the pain of constant effort, accompanied by trust in people and the cosmos. Engaged cosmology, in turn, will give birth to new possibilities for freedom and a world of planetary peace. As theologian Mary Grey asserts, "Justice is the very heart of God; it arises from the divine vision for the restored and transformed universe." Seen this way, engaged action, conscience, and consciousness are one: together they comprise a seamless garment that is engaged cosmology.

Engaged cosmology culminates as a spectrum theology
of contemplation, liberation and creation theologies.
Each of these spiritualities not only have their
distinct validity but also continually interact in new
and creative ways.

—*Rosemary Radford Ruether*

The Path Before Us

Skies open.
Panoramas emerge.
The universe appears
enveloped in incandescent hope.
With fresh energy
we transcend the inertia of the day
and rediscover love
pulsating from within the cosmos's hidden heart.

Steadfast Patience

It comes only to those who live as though eternity stretches before them,
carefree, silent and endless. I learn it daily, learn it with many poems,
for which I am grateful. Patience is all.

—*Rainer Maria Rilke*

From engaging, our imagination is awakened and new relationships develop. Steadfast and patient, we stand tall in the face of reactionary trends; we embrace the New Story as with renewed energy we invigorate our journey and reinvent our life from within the context of the universe itself.

With this in mind, we see the whole world as sacred and sacramental, an incarnational event. Enfolded in this great embrace we are one with all and yet distinct. We discover that the divine is always manifesting in the particularity of matter; each moment a new incarnation invites us forward into life. We are invited to savour and celebrate the beauty available to us in an emerging universe that unites us to the God of all that is; we are a part of this unfolding universe.

Always in search of more, looking toward the future with a sense of hope, we look around us with awe and wonder as our hearts are healed and our spirits soar. From this cosmic perspective we view the beauty and brokenness of life: the tragedy of poverty, the loss of species, the melting icecaps, but also the eagle soaring free, acts of anonymous generosity. Each moment, tragic or joyful, creeps into our consciousness and permeates the depths of our soul.

With this new awareness we feel the pain of tsunamis and hurricanes, and the nobility of those who transcend grief and greed. We embrace each other in acts of courageous solidarity to heal our hearts and bind up the wounds of our broken world. Only then will we find peace, tranquility, and clarity.

The passing days are marked by new cultural moments: breaking down the barriers of structural oppression, searching for wisdom within, expanding our horizons to the far reaches of the universe. We strive again and again to heal what is broken and renew the face of the earth. In this enduring and prolonged quest, we experience divinity in every molecule of existence and look for sacredness in each day's struggles.

We rediscover how the universe sustains us in our quest. Each revelatory moment enhances our capacity to act, each lesson from tradition promotes our ability to trust, and each watershed event in our story contains new wisdom to illuminate our path.

Through an integration of these narratives, which in fact are one, we gain access to our life and the trajectory that lies before us on the way.

> Miracles happen.
> Emergent songs appear.
> Fire illuminates the sky.
> Structures of oppression dissolve,
> Exposed by the radiance of the sun.
> Once more
> we embrace the earth as one.
> The fresh energy of humanity
> springs forth from the risen heart
> of the universe,
> and we once again pursue
> the world for which we are waiting,
> a world of gratitude and love.
> Each creature is an amplifier and enhancement
> of sacredness and depth
> during these turbulent moments
> in our brokenhearted world.

A Call to Engagement

> *The two stars are in the process of coming together through the ascent of matter and the descent of God. The impersonal cosmos and the personal God are uniting … the human efforts to build a society of love, justice and understanding are all parts of a single cosmic process.*
>
> —*Thomas King, SJ*

We stand on the verge of a transitional moment so vast and all embracing that it has profound implications for culture, psychology, politics, and, in particular, economics. We need to be grounded in a spirituality that will provide wider horizons, greater understanding, and guidance for the future; a spirituality that is counter cultural; a spirituality that stands over against the view that economics is the "operative theology" of society. We need to celebrate community and develop a world view that unites mind and matter, that generates hope that another world is possible. Some call this the Ecozoic Age; others name it the reign of God.

Our new world view is enhanced and communicated by the stories that give direction to our lives, shape our sense of the sacred, nurture values, and appreciate life. We are called to celebrate that another world is possible, a world that sees community as the relationship of the human and non-human world, a world made up of a community of communities, a world that is decentralized, a world in which change is possible and sustainability a guiding force. As Thomas Berry puts it, "Those overarching movements … give shape and meaning to life by relating the human venture to the larger destinies of the universe. The Great Work now is to carry out the transition from a period of human devastation of the Earth to a period when humans would be present to the planet in a mutually enhancing manner."

A Window of Gratitude and Grace

> *If the only prayer you ever say is thank you that will suffice.*
>
> —*Meister Eckhart*

As I sit here at St. Peter's Seminary, in London, Ontario and gaze out at the snow-carpeted campus before me, I am amazed and grateful. Amazed that after all these years I have returned to this place of so many memories, to share my journey with others and to listen to their stories. It never occurred to me that the privilege of this moment would occur.

When I listen closely, I hear a song, a melody of gratitude for all creation, shouting a proclamation of beauty, telling tales of wonder, stories of incarnation, narratives of gratitude and hope. As I look out the window, my vision expands; it is as if my view of the campus becomes a window on the world, a window of gratitude through which to view those moments of grace that have blessed my life.

And so I celebrate with gratitude

- The love of a French-Canadian mother and father of Irish ancestry whose love and generosity gave life to my sister, my brother, and me.

- The bioregion of the earth on which I was born, with its beauty, river, trees, seasons, and farms.

- The two-room schoolhouse where I began my education and the teachers, classrooms, and baseball fields that taught me many lessons of life.

- My parents' Christian faith, which they practiced and passed on to me by example.

- The moments of grace that occurred through the study of chemistry, theology, philosophy, social science, culture, and spirituality.

- The people in my life, both mentors and friends, who have contributed to my desire to escape the "unlived life."

- My introduction to the wonders of a magnificent universe that continues to evoke and support my deepest passion for life.

- All who have been "listening hearts" in my life and who have confirmed my belief in the presence of God in all things.

From my window on the world here in the early years of the twenty-first century, I see that a new moment is upon us. From the SROs (single rooms only) in San Francisco and across this great continent, in community centers, churches, and other gathering places, a new cultural impulse is formed. Among the homeless, the displaced persons everywhere, and those who work to meet their immediate needs (food, shelter, clothing, healthcare), an enticing texture of joyous service is palpable and hovers in the air. From a puzzling paradox of affluence and poverty, influence and powerlessness, a fresh perception of beauty shines forth. These people without an address have taken out a long-term lease on the heart of America. Those unable to ever utter the words "I'm going home" remind us that the only abiding home any of us truly possesses is the shelter of the heart.

These are "companions on the way," people of the inner city whose shattered lives and broken dreams are metaphors for the failed experiment of the American Empire. Yet their beauty and their brokenness resonate in our psyches and the traditions that we hold dear: "I was hungry ... as often you did it to the least of my people, you did it to me."

From the inner cities of our nation to the pulpits and town meetings, a new surge of prophecy and protest is rising among us. From a tsunami of grief, new waves of hope are rising in the hearts of the people, a gathering of fresh energy and moral outrage designed to stop the train wreck of broken lives and the destruction of a nation openly betraying its founding principles and abandoning its leadership role on the world stage.

A new wave of hope is gathering on the shore of our psyches; it will quench our collective thirst for justice and moisten the roots of a new world view, a new story, a better way, breaking on the shores of this new moment. As we review our journey and reflect on our lives during these darkest of days, we discover hope in this struggle and gratitude for the courage, creativity, and joy that will fuel the journey and provide fresh energy for the challenges and opportunities that lie ahead.

The Monks of Skid Row

A strange breed of monks, these 12,000 derelicts of life,
These lovable genial isolated human beings
They live with a past not to be forgotten,
A present built out of isolation,
And a future that promises and hopes for nothing.
These monks of the inner city are more alone
Than the strictest contemplative...
And often more redeemed
As they traffic in their currency of cigarettes,
Where to get beer, a bed, a meal, a job and sometimes money,
They are selfless and concerned.
These islands of humanity boasting of a day's work.

And regretting a wasted life.

They trust NO ONE as they walk.
Their silent world of pain and fear,
This order of the street, men without futures, without rights.
Poor, pushed, passed by and possessed by those who provide beds
and food,
Keeping them on one aimless treadmill of life.
They live without solutions,
With no one listening to what they say,
No one asking them to talk,
Inviting them to spill, to drain
The poison from their lives,
A poison that festers in nightmares, alcohol,
Fear of work, passive acceptance of mistreatment, unexpressed
anger and fear.

2

Epic of Engagement

"The starry sky is like a city by night ... the stars are like streets."
— *Ernesto Cardinal*

For the Children

Kathy Kelly, Nobel Peace Prize nominee and founder of Voices in the Wilderness, is a prophet for the "little ones," the children of Iraq. She tells of a time the children were reluctant to go to bed although the hour was late. As the bullets cracked in the night sky, Kathy made her plea that it was bedtime. "You can finish your game in the morning," she told them. The children responded, as with one voice, "But, Miss, we may not be here in the morning."

It is a terrible truth: the children of Iraq are in danger. So are the children of the First World countries who breathe auto exhaust and are surrounded by industrial pollution. On our planet, 80 percent of all illness is attributed to polluted water. No wonder potable water is often called blue gold. Whether from war, pollution, or poverty, the hope of the world and the future of the little ones is now at a crossroads.

When asked why he had devoted his life to creating a more viable planetary home, geologian and cultural historian Thomas Berry replied, "I do it for children." We would do well to emulate his example.

New Day

Separation opens to mystery
And lets wisdom in
While echoes of former pain

Greet a transparent sky.
From the depths
Our spirits rise
To greet a new era
And welcome a new day.

For the World

The goal of this quest is earth healing, a healed relationship between
men and women, between humans and the earth.

—*Rosemary Radford Ruether*

There were thousands of victims of the December 2004 tsunami in East Asia, and approximately one-half million survivors were left without food, water, and shelter. At the same time malls in the West filled with holiday shoppers. Life goes on. People are arrested in Boston as they protest the closing of a parish church that has been their spiritual home for a lifetime. Soldiers and civilians die as the occupying forces prepare again to impose their political system on an ancient culture. Corporate officers betray their responsibilities out of personal greed. Politicians spin the facts until truth itself is another casualty of the culture.

As the children of the baby boomers move into leadership, they inherit a failed structure now in its terminal phase. The desire of the human heart is once more broken by unmet needs of dying institutions and a disoriented world that has lost its inner compass and is spinning wildly off course.

In the developing world people live longer and have bigger homes, yet we have aching hearts. We feel deceived by media that propagate deception and false promises. We are terrorized by the impending end of lives that feel profoundly unfulfilled and unfinished. Bewildered and betrayed, we struggle to find meaning and a purpose for our lives.

We realize – if we allow ourselves to do so – that our lives and our country have been party to a grand deception. The crisis is rooted in how we have located ourselves in the world and our experience of meaning and depth. We become aware of the magnitude of the crisis and its powerful impact on our lives. As a result, we hunger for fresh perspectives and new beginnings; during this uncertain time we yearn for promise and possibility in our future. This search for a new perspective invites both a recollection of the past and a vision of a hope-filled tomorrow.

As I reflect on the decades that have passed, I remember the hopes and promises that accompanied many of those days. Our fondest hopes seemed possible, and the strategic approaches we employed held the promise of the realization of our most treasured dreams. We believed that a better world was possible and that we could work together to bring it about. We dreamed of Camelot, and we believed in our dream.

As we move into the second decade of the twenty-first century, we need to draw on the universe's engaged wisdom to find our path and to make our world a safer and more peaceful place.

Healing Our Brokenheartedness

This intimacy exists with the stars in the heavens and with the flowering forms of earth, this presence of humans with other members of the animal world is unique.

—Thomas Berry

The world lies shrouded in pain; the fundamental purpose of its peoples and creatures is confused by the ashes of possession that anesthetize – although never completely – the hunger for the divine.

At this moment we are being encouraged by the cosmos and invited by the Divine to authenticate our quest, to understand that the distortions of corporate greed and the intoxication of misguided mysticism are echoes of our desire to come home. With this in mind we realize that our abiding desires for peace and geo-justice are manifestations of our genetic coding to be at one with all that is, to come home to our God.

As I reflect on my journey into justice-making, direct service, communications therapy, community organization, conscientization, geo-justice, and engaged (community) cosmology, I realize that each step moved toward increased intimacy and experience of the divine embrace. Perhaps due to my avoidance of the responsibility of intimacy or my embarrassment and fear of mysticism and genuine discomfort with God-talk, I have in the past skated over the implications of my spiritual journey. I can now view my journey into justice-making as a movement toward the kingdom of God on Earth, a planetary Pentecost in which a community of justice and peace is a new moment of "realized eschatology," a new moment when heaven happens now and our God becomes more present and palpable in our midst.

In light of this realization, I now return to my journey and reflect on how each step has been a response to an invitation and has resulted in an ever-deepening awareness of an ongoing call from the heart of the Divine.

Beauty and Balance

There arises a spirituality in which the human city and healthy conditions of natural life are also to be brought together in harmony.
—*Leonardo Boff*

The great work of justice-making is a spiritual practice; justice calls us to respond to the divine invitation to make heaven happen now, to celebrate our immersion in the Divine, and to understand each act of justice-making as a step toward making the kingdom present in our midst. As we search for the engaged wisdom, poised on the precipice of a brokenhearted world, we discover that the great work of justice-making is perhaps our most profound prayer. Through acts of justice-making we participate in bringing about a planetary Pentecost; we fashion a community of life flourishing with beauty, integrity, and balance. We celebrate the reign of God in our midst, a culminating celebration of

- communications therapy as the process of delivering a person to himself or herself;
- organization as the first act of justice-making, new life burgeoning in our minds and in our midst;
- conscientization as an incarnational moment that celebrates the newness bursting forth in the hearts and minds of the people as well as in each flower, bird, and river in the gallery of beauty that is God's creation;
- geo-justice as a paschal mystery story that unfolds in the engaged wisdom proclaimed from the heart of divinity and echoes in the far reaches of the world;
- engaged cosmology as the context for all our journeys and the womb from which justice is born. From here the reign of God appears, a planetary Pentecost erupts among us, and beauty shines forth enveloped in justice.

Our acts of justice-making flood us with new energy. We feel growing affinity for and meaning being revealed to us. Everything – cricket, ant, tree, and human – is a book about God. The incarnation is present among us; birth continues, flowers bloom, puppies are born, morning comes, and ideas and projects are brought into existence. Bethlehem encompasses us in a multitude of ways, and its diversity astonishes us with beauty, blessing, and new life. We make our Easter with Earth and every species. Interiority indicates our origins and our story, the place of depth, the Grand Canyon of our souls. In pain, letting go happens and death has meaning. Communion points toward inter-connectedness and the divine spirit from which trans-formation comes – the energy that weaves social and ecological concerns into a seamless garment of balance, of geo-justice.

Astonished by dreams that originate in our imagination and provide starting points of hope, and enchanted by their story, we see our prophetic acts as expressions of the pulsating heart of the universe. We remember ecstatic moments – sunset, mountain, meal, river, meadow, or night sky – that liberated our hearts.

Turbulence

Turbulent wisdom
emanates from the stars
as deep desires boil over
into love.
Encounters of transparency
reveal vulnerable souls
as we wrestle in communion
with our creator God.
Genetic memories unfold,
activating the heart
while once more stories are told
with the universe in mind.

Touchstones on the Journey

Anyone who attempts to act and do for others, or for the world without deepening his or her own self understanding. Freedom, integrity, capac-ity to love, will not have anything to give to others.

—*Thomas Merton*

This work was born from reflection on the narratives that have shaped my sense of the sacred. With the benefit of time, I have come to acknowledge these stories as turning points and/or defining moments in my life and sometimes within the wider world. Living in a fragmented world, I have participated in activities that hold out the promise of new life. At this stage of my journey I feel moved to look back over my life and the waves that have carried me to this moment and to explore the relationship between these cultural moments and my faith tradition.

My intention is to search for parallel themes in the approaches of cosmology, spiritual tradition, and the narrative of action in the world. My hope is that an integration of these approaches will both heal the fragmentation within and point toward further engagement that will culminate in a strategic synthesis appropriately responsive to the needs of this critical moment. I believe that we will hear and respond to the call to integration in a fragmented world when we are able to discover how each source of wisdom has contributed to and animated our journey. Thus the goal of these pages is to discover how the synthesis of these approaches can be a synthesis of uncommon wisdom and a resource for enacting the new epic of society and cosmos. The result will be an integral approach, empowering and advancing societal transformation and enhancing the health of our planetary home.

Autumn's Wisdom

Autumn's wordless wisdom
Speaks to me of death
While the glory of each fall leaf
Evokes a silhouette of life.

Our Faith Tradition

I am a pilgrim of the future on my way back from a journey
made entirely in the past.

—*Pierre Teilhard de Chardin*

Our faith tradition is integrally connected to our actions in the world. These actions can be understood as both sacred and earthly – bringing justice to the world so every part of creation can achieve its full potential. Our faith tradition helps us identify more fully with the earth and its peoples as we work to birth a new creation of love, justice, confidence, and trust. Efforts to birth new creation require that we aid communication as we give witness to what we believe is true from the revelation found in scripture and in the natural world. We will also develop local communities that engage in cooperative initiatives and we will serve them as motivators, analysts, and constructive critics of the process. All the while, we will develop a dynamic theology of engaged cosmology that offers new hope and possibilities for everyone.

This process is described well for Christians by Pierre Teilhard de Chardin, who wrote,

> I believe that the universe is an evolution.
> I believe that evolution proceeds through the spirit.
> I believe that spirit is fully realized in a form of personality.
> I believe that the supremely personal is the universal Christ.

In June of 2005, representatives of the Brothers of Earth and the Sisters of Earth, women and men whose lives are inspired by a spirituality of Earth, gathered in Poughkeepsie, New York, at the grave of Teilhard de Chardin to mark the fiftieth anniversary of his death.

Pierre Teilhard de Chardin, SJ, was a great bridge builder for our time. He was a priest, theologian, scientist, and prophetic voice. Through his writings, in particular his signature works *The Human Phenomenon* and *The Divine Milieu*, he brought Christian faith and evolutionary science into a unified vision. He was a man of great courage, deep devotion, and much love. His writings are primary resources in our search to understand the origins of the universe, its unfolding in time, and humanity's place within it.

I have observed both in my life and in the lives of others a profound connection between peoples' engagement in projects of change and their relationship to their faith tradition. This connection is sometimes explicit and conscious to people who are currently practicing their faith; for others, the connection may be preconscious or more hidden and oblique. In either case it is my conviction that our faith tradition has a profound impact on our actions in the world. This is not easy to prove empirically, of course, but I believe it is demonstrated in many ways.

Beatitudes for the New Creation

Blessed are the hopeful, they hold a promise of tomorrow.

Blessed are the courageous, they embrace the challenge of today.

Blessed are the forgiving, they are free of the burden of the past.

Blessed are the people of prolonged engagement, they will create a better world for the children.

Blessed are the disappointed, they will rise and anticipate a better day.

Blessed are the self-forgetful, they will engage in a compassionate embrace.

Blessed are the flowers, bursting forth in the spring.

Blessed are the children, celebrating spontaneity and new life.

Blessed are the contemplatives, they will embrace the universe as one.

Blessed are the liberators, they will set all the captives free.

Blessed are the creation-centered people, they will appreciate the beauty of the earth.

Blessed are the engaged mystics, they will ignite a fire on the earth and unite the stars and the street.

3

The Great "I Ams"

The 'I am' that one says the oneself is as concrete as the circulation of one's blood.

—Mary Caroline Richards

Each of us has a core set of beliefs about who and what and why we are. We seldom reflect on these beliefs, and even less frequently do we articulate them. I have thought long and hard about these realities of self, so to speak, and finally was able to write my own set of "I ams":

I am stardust flowing out of the heart of divinity. I am who I am; it is by being who I am that I discover my authentic identity. I am called into intimacy, energetic love, and an ever-deepening capacity to embrace and celebrate my as-yet-unlived life. I am called out of the fetal waters of fear, doubt, repression, and hesitation to be reborn as a new me, a new relationship, a new life, a new plant, a new "I am." I am invited to live in a world that is inclusive, a place of belonging that empowers me and others, that celebrates accomplishments, that is fueled by hope, and that is identified by the touchstone categories of reciprocity and mutual enhancement. I am summoned to participate in the reinvention of humanity, to confront this withering moment in history with freedom and courage and an ever-deepening capacity to bring forth a world that is not yet but will become.

Culture: Personal Story

The world today is on the verge of a new age and a new culture.

—Bede Griffiths

Going into therapy involves a struggle to unravel past experiences and become liberated from internal forces that threaten our creative energies. It is an open-ended adventure. Although it involves risk and pain, it is also an opportunity to heal past wounds and realize increased potential.

Prompted by the turbulence of the times and the upheavals within church and society, I went into therapy. I was searching for validation of my story up to that point in my life. I felt a growing sense of fragmentation within and alienation without. Looking back in light of the universe story and the creation stories of Genesis, I realize that I sought to discover my identity, to discover what it means to be human. In other words, what is my story? In what way does it need to be healed? Should it be celebrated? Telling my story in the therapeutic context was encouraging. I found that storytelling fueled and energized my hope-filled quest for relationship and community. Others reported the same experience

As we remember and recount our story we discover the self-healing properties of our psyche; we discover that our psyche is both co-extensive with the universe and a context for adventure and celebration. We connect our story to the unfolding events of the universe and gain a greater appreciation for the beauty and pain that permeate the cosmos and our soul through moments of genesis and transformation. As we embrace the cosmic dimension of our story, the barriers to mysticism melt and we begin to experience in a more profound way how our story is indeed an important paragraph in the Great Story, a story also told each day by the sunlight and darkness, river and ice floe, child and crocus.

The story of the birth of the cosmos has been told in many ways. One of the most impressive is "The Creation" by James Weldon Johnson:

> And God stepped out on space
> And he looked around and said:
> I'm lonely –
> I'll make me a world.
> And far as the eye of God could see
> Darkness covered everything,
> Blacker than a hundred midnights
> Down in a cypress swamp.
> Then God smiled,
> And the light broke,
> And the darkness rolled up on one side,

And the light stood shining on the other,
And God said: That's good!
. . . .
And there the great God almighty, ...
Who rounded the earth in the middle of his hand;
This great God,
Like a mammy bending over her baby,
Kneeled down in the dust
Toiling over a lump of clay
Till he shaped it in his own image;
Then into it he blew the breath of life,
And man became a living soul.
Amen. Amen.

A Time to Change

Metaphorically, it is as if we have entered into the dark space of the cosmic confessional and have been given a new perspective. One which absolves us of all notions of ourselves as separate from the entire cosmic and planetary process through which we have come and of which we are a part.

—Gail Worcelo, SGM

Between the vision and the act lies the shadow.

—T.S. Eliot

The decades that preceded these early years of the new millennium have been filled with turbulence. Each one has been marked with its own cultural moments. The 1960s witnessed the civil rights movement, the Vietnam War, and Vatican Council II. These years were characterized by promise and upheaval. In the 1970s people reacted to the resistance they encountered when attempting to bring about structural change. Their struggle brought some people to therapy. They felt, "If I can't change the world, I will change myself."

I was one of those people. Suddenly everything I believed in was called into question. I wasn't sure what I had achieved in the past had any value – and unsure about what I was called to in the future. The present was chaos;

my life lacked order and direction. I began communications therapy. Like many others with similar backgrounds and aspirations, I was struggling to deal with the lifestyle implications that were implicit in the changes of the 1960s and 1970s. I gathered weekly with many priests and sisters to try to make sense of my life and the emotional antecedents that had contributed to the confusion that I felt. A desire to connect my inner journey with the quest for social change was active in my therapeutic quest. This attempt to bring my two worlds together has remained an enduring pursuit to today. If the goal of therapy can be understood as delivering a person to himself or herself, this new capacity for fulfillment will contribute to the integration of consciousness and conscience and enhance the capacity for an integrated life.

It was inspired by a founding vision articulated in Robert Linders' book *Prescription for Rebellion*. He asserted that personal and emotional processes are the instruments of cultural evolution. The hoped-for result would be an "environment of friendship," a movement that would contribute to the "making of a counter culture." The work of communication therapy, beginning with emotional struggles, would often evoke a profound spiritual experience; the book by Ralph Waldo Trine entitled *In Tune with the Infinite* provided language and focus for these cosmic ecstatic moments. He wrote:

> Within yourself lies the cause of Whatever enters into your life. To come into full realization of your own awakened interior powers, is to be able to condition your life in exact accord with what you would have it – the power that moves and holds the stars in their courses, illumines, sustains and fights for the brave and the upright. To ally ourselves with it is the secret of all real and satisfying living – mutuality is the law of life, and through it and it alone can we fulfill our highest destiny – the realization of undreamed powers.

Therapy can also be understood as a process that frees us from the forces that drain our creative energies. To engage in therapy is to cast oneself on the waters of life and thereby live a fuller and more responsible life. By resolving the confusion in our inner life, our participation in the world can become more effective and fruitful.

Therapy taught me a great deal. I learned that I can be healed, that therapy is a way to enhance communication and increase self-esteem. I learned that insight into my emotional life is necessary if I am going to confront structures of oppression, and that it is important not to act out my emotional life in the theatre of social change. I learned that the search for personal health and healing cannot be accomplished at the expense of my commitment to justice and change.

I learned that a search for that last "neurotic nugget" is a deceptive goal in life: one can spend too much time and energy in search of emotional health. I also learned that emotional health and responsibility for one's life takes struggle and a strong desire for fulfillment. I learned that therapy is not a passive act where we simply become unengaged recipients of change.

I learned that there is a profound connection between the emotional life and our actions in the world. I learned that therapy requires responsibility and courage, struggle and risk. I learned that the emotional journey is an ongoing process. I learned that therapy is not a way of life but rather a means to living. And I learned that healing is a continuous process and that the beauty of creation and encounters with the natural world can help make us whole again.

Communications therapy as a process can be summarized by this brief poem by Rumi. This thirteenth-century Persian Sufi poet and mystic is one of the most widely read poets today. He was a man of tremendous creative energy, and his words remain alive across space and time into our own day. His words open the heart to mystery, connect us to the cosmos, and bring joy and depth to our journey with the Ultimate.

> Move from within.
> Don't move the way
> Fear wants you to.

Living out those words is difficult and rewarding. I learned that in therapy my anger at the system may be, at least in part, displaced anger from unresolved childhood issues. As a child I was separated from my mother because she became ill. At the time I felt my own life was in danger, that I was being separated from the source of life itself. Now, as an adult, I have felt echoes of that early separation when a relationship ended, my health was endangered, or my livelihood was uncertain.

I ask myself: What do I do in the face of personal threat or loss? How can I respond creatively to lack of gratitude for my efforts, to feeling unexpected violation or betrayal, to character and "soul" assassination? How do I expose my wounds without imposing blame? I don't yet have clear answers to these questions. But one lesson I have learned is that many events of life and the behaviour of others are beyond my control. I am not in charge.

My response to the personal or communal injustice that causes me pain is to make every effort to transform whatever patterns of oppression I recognize. I strive to respond with all the strength, wisdom, and insight I can muster. Initially I give myself permission to express outrage at the injustices that come my way, and yet, simultaneously, in the deepest way possible, I try to let go of how these events invaded my life. I acknowledge my pain and remain grounded in my trust that clarity and direction will emerge out of the turbulence, that in the larger picture justice will reign. Saul Alinsky writes, "the action is in the reaction."

When faced with unpredictable events that churn our emotions, it is important to stay grounded. Our primary spiritual practice becomes one of staying in touch with our deepest self; receiving the support of friends, family, and nature; and acknowledging our immersion in the divine embrace that reminds us of love, trust, and the possibility of a better tomorrow.

We let go of the past and take up the challenge to move forward and begin again. We recover from the shattering of our plans and perceptions to experience more profoundly than ever before the new possibilities that await us. Perhaps the new millennium truly will be a time of grace and the twenty-first century a revolutionary event in all our lives. Despite the planetary crisis that confronts us, we emerge with a renewed sense of the sacred as we move forward and engage in the soul-work that can make the new millennium the place of the planetary Pentecost.

From Turbulence to Transformation

We are people of the story ordained to celebrate the liturgy of life in the process of creating a Third Testament.

—Miriam Therese Winter

The journey of a soul in transition can feel like a ride down a turbulent river. The soul is sometimes submerged, gasping for air, swirling out of control. Yet when we let go and trust the deepest current of life, we find that even in the most chaotic waters of change there is always buoyancy and that the water is fertile with the promise of new birth. Personal crisis always holds the possibility of passage to a new level of maturity, to a more compassionate ground of living. Successfully navigating these turbulent waters of transition requires accessing the wisdom of the past and preparing to meet the challenges of the future while responding fully and creatively to the present moment of grace held within the crisis. What is true of personal times of transition is also true in social and communal crisis. Within each turbulent eddy of crisis there is a still-point of grace, a point for pondering the divine presence and gathering our resources to stay afloat. In this still-point we realize that we are not alone as we ride the rapids of change and transition. We realize that we can form networks that are vehicles for relationships as well as interconnecting webs that keep us all afloat.

We come together to discover our allies, identify our strengths, explore our potential for growth, review our vision, and develop strategies for coping with change. We realize that we are not passive riders, that we can actually affect the course of our journey. When we come together for information and support, we listen to one another's voices, reflect on our inner promptings, and adjust our course. This process enables us to look toward the future with hope – a future that will be realized from within the ever-expanding constellation of relationships and support.

In the still-point we become aware not only of our mutual support but also of the Spirit, who sustains us and provides us with a vision of the possible to guide us on our journey. In this divine buoyancy we realize that accomplishing the work of transition requires tolerance for turbulence and uncertainty along with radical trust that balance and direction will come out of what appears to be chaos. From this place of ambiguity and emerging order we continue Christ's work of shaping a shared destiny of planetary liberation and profound fulfillment, a process referred to as the coming of Christ's reign. This work of transition can be accomplished only when it is nourished by an intimate experience of the Divine. Only when our individual and corporate efforts are grounded in God can we summon the necessary courage and strength to achieve that which appears impossible – the great work of realizing the historic mission of humanity as we usher in the age of justice, peace, and integrity of creation.

This new world view and the strategies and tactics that accompany its application are born out of the collective imaginations of scientists, artists, theologians, and activists, among others. When all of us listen and respond together to divine revelation as it is expressed in traditional ways, through creation and within the human spirit, these new understandings will extend into cultural transformation. As we listen to the voices of the earth, we take up the enormous challenges of restructuring education, religion, and public and corporate life with a goal of ushering Earth and all its peoples into an era of harmony and peace.

To bring about and maintain this new era will require decisive and collaborative action; the magnitude of the task will require a community of creative and dedicated people whose diverse backgrounds and gifts will be brought into focus by a transcendent and common goal. As we engage in change, each moment of transition evokes memories of what has gone before; we feel gratitude for all we have received.

Simultaneously, the waters of transition invite us to embrace the future. During this daring and delicate time of moving into an unknown future, those engaged in this great adventure will empower us to withstand the predictable accusations, innuendos, and half-truths of those who cling to the status quo. Resistance calls us to return to the still-point of grace wherein we seek the Divine and struggle to transcend our own ego-involvement and self-delusion. It is here, in the fertile womb of silence, that the new vision is rekindled, that we will discover our place and path in the larger drama of life.

The entire process of the soul in a time of such transition is focused and stabilized through connecting with trusted colleagues and doing everything possible to capture each precious moment as an opportunity to ignite a new consciousness, a new culture.

At all times on this immense journey we will be energized by gratitude and freed by the capacity to surrender any impulse to dominate or control. Only then will the divine plan reveal itself in mysterious and powerful ways; only then will those engaged in the journey of transition be able to access the capacity to endure this profound period of growth, decline, and renewal; only then will we be energized to move into the reign of God.

Involvement in this prophetic effort will stretch the envelope of our imagination for what is possible. It will thrust us into a future where there is full congruence between authority and self-initiative, vision and practice, lifestyle and engaged spirituality, personal integrity and professional responsibility. Leadership will demonstrate a healthy disregard for status or stature. Each person will place performance over ego, continuity over chaos, trust over suspicion, gratitude over greed. Only in this way will it be possible to design and develop the delicate and prophetic vehicles necessary for the task.

As participants in this great transformation, we cannot stand outside the changes we strive to work toward. The unfolding future will invite us to new promise and participation, new commitment and collegiality. As we accompany one another into the era of consciousness and culture, we will move forward in hope that the future will be better than the past. In this new era engaged wisdom will be fostered and life affirmed on many levels.

The goal of our journey will become clearer – to liberate ourselves and all involved from personal oppression and the structures of domination. As we are inspired by a glimpse of newfound freedom and aroused by the struggle for fulfillment on a personal and cultural level, each of us will embrace this new moment of grace and respond with rigorous effort and engaged cosmology.

Strengthened by the mental discipline and a willingness to embrace the magnitude of the task, convinced that each of us and our collective efforts are indeed "bathed in God," we will move forward fully prepared to exercise the courage needed to create a vital constellation of functional relationships. Each of us will take up the challenge that is based on truth, conscious of the past and predicted in the vision of an enchanting future. We can take our anthem from the words of Meister Eckhart:

> When I was born
> All Creation stood up and shouted
> There is God
> And they were correct.

With gratitude and grace we celebrate the story of creation, liberation and us.

Prayer

> What is more ordinary
> Than prayer
> Each moment
> Inaugurates a breath
> The inhalation, and
> Exaltation
> of existence

Each moment
An invitation, to
Pay attention, to
The wordless silence
Of the earth

Each moment
A choir of adoration
A song of beauty

The frog plays bass,
The cricket tenor
Each a subject of the song
A chorus of beauty
A proclamation
A cosmic melody …
An ordinary prayer

4

Passion, Risk and Patterns of Meaning

With what shall I come before the LORD ....
He has told you, O mortal, what is good;
and what does the LORD require of you
but to do justice, and to love kindness,
and to walk humbly with your God?

—Micah 6:6-8

In my life's journey I've come to accept that death and births are intimately connected, that fear and fulfillment are two faces of one act. I now know that self-expression

- does not cause death but life;

- does not diminish but expands;

- does not threaten but encourages;

- does not repress but liberates; and

- does not plunder but praises.

As I see my journey within the larger pattern of existence, my fear is transformed into fulfillment and transformation, repression into freedom, despair into hope, and death into a threshold of new life. I proclaim a new epic of engagement, celebrate beauty, arise to new life, commune with the sacred, ingest life's mystery, and pay attention to the wonder of solidarity and hope.

Social organization

When I grew impatient with the growing disparity between institutional agendas and the deep knowing of the people of God, I went to the streets. I listened to the needs of the people. I was determined to empower them to act and to resolve the issues that were their greatest concern. In the same way the voices and actions of the prophets gave expression to projects of justice and protest. Today, society finds expression through social organizing intended to transform concerns into cultural change.Organization is the first act of justice-making.

Saul Alinsky speaks with wisdom of the scope of justice-making:

All I know is what every good organizer knows ... you react to all the action with a reflex. If a man has opportunity and the power to use that opportunity, then I'll bet on him to cross any bridge, no matter how tough or seemingly hopeless it may look. As a mat-ter of fact, I've already bet my life on it.

Movements in the culture increased my restlessness and I increasingly reflected on and engaged in acts of justice-making through organization. My work – viewed within the originating energy of the universe and the prophetic voices of scripture – began to focus more and more on bringing people together to listen to one another, to decide on the issues to address, and to take action to bring about the desired changes.

Questions about justice have been the most engaging and sometimes the most puzzling of my life. On occasion I have asked myself whether my Irish heritage, widely known for being anti-government and resilient in the face of oppression, has contributed to my impulse to work for the underdog, to be on the side of the poor. Whatever the reason, I have always found myself aligned with the marginalized and disadvantaged.

When the Latin American bishops proposed that the work of theol-ogy must be done with a preferential option for the poor, they made a monumental contribution to the work of liberation and justice. The phrase certainly resonated with me personally. The ecological devastation in our day has convinced me that the option for the poor needs to be extended to the poor earth. The potential for an environmental wasteland has given a new meaning to poverty. It has been my experience, however, that justice is not well understood in relationship to the new way of seeing the world. Not only are we troubled by the pain of social and ecological injustice, but we are also troubled by the approaches taken to heal injustice.

Approaches to social justice have remained embedded in the distortion of our redemption-centered culture. Many who become engaged in work for justice burn out and leave the work, very discouraged. Guilt and a misguided obligation have parched their spirit and contracted their vision. On occasion, they sacrificed their marriages or their personal health on the altar of community concerns. The work for justice can itself become an act of injustice.

Much justice work also has overlooked the interior life. Justice workers often do not feel nourished in their efforts to liberate the oppressed. Friends and colleagues have often reported that striving for social justice left them fragmented and alienated. Given this experience, they retreated. But work for justice can be different. The key is compassion. It can best be understood in relationship to the universe as an intimate presence and a response to the supreme challenge of extending love and relationship to self, others, and Earth.

I remember an event that marked the beginnings of my organizing experience. My older brother was the best pitcher on our baseball team. I wasn't playing much, so he and I convinced our manager that I should catch when he pitched. This was my first organizing project, my first experience of being involved in shifting patterns of relationship to achieve a desired result.

Later, as a student with the Industrial Areas Foundation / Saul Alinsky Training Institute, I became excited about the opportunity of learning more about how to empower the poor and disadvantaged. Remembering how I solved the problem of not playing enough on my local baseball team, I applied what I had learned to my justice work. I looked for others with whom to play the game of justice – people with influence to whom I could listen and with whom I could work.

I look across my office and glance at the words inscribed in a frame hanging on the wall. They read:

> Life is an adventure of passion, risk,
> danger, laughter, beauty, love,
> A burning curiosity to go with the action
> To see what it is all about,
> To search for a pattern of meaning,
> To burn one's bridges because you're never going
> to go back anyway…

These words, creatively inscribed in calligraphy, are the words of Saul Alinsky. I met Alinsky in Chicago while I was a student with the Industrial Areas Foundation/Saul Alinsky Training Institute in the early 1970s. Alinsky was the founder of a powerful social movement that changed political activism in North America, a revolutionary event that brought together labour unions, the community, and the church.

The work of Saul Alinsky made inroads in my soul; he was committed to people, to justice, and to the eradication of poverty and powerlessness. I felt privileged to join his work to support people in their struggle for dignity, destiny, and the ability to act. It was a great adventure, an adventure that I now see as a significant part of the journey from the stars to the streets.

Alinsky taught many lessons: be creative, continue to question, be flexible, trust in the goodness of people, and always believe in a better tomorrow. His credo could be stated in this way: "Love your neighbour. All people are created equal. You are each other's keeper."

Over the years the lessons I learned from Saul Alinsky and the universality of his ideas were indelibly printed in my mind. His insights into purpose, power, education, and communication, and the strategies and tactics he developed in his books *Reveille for Radicals* and *Rules for Radicals*, are integral to the practice of engaged cosmology. His vision of a second revolution, a revolution for meaning and purpose, is a revolution of the soul. In the closing chapter of *Rules for Radicals* he wrote: "When Americans can no longer see the stars, the times are tragic. We must believe that it is the darkness before the dawn of a beautiful new world; we will see it when we believe it."

I remain grateful to the vision of Saul Alinsky. Perhaps inspired by his vision we will once again see the stars, and they will illuminate the streets of our cities and the dawn of a beautiful new world will truly be realized.

My experience in community organization was liberating. In Toronto a delegation of community people went to City Hall to meet with the commissioner of public works. This man had consistently refused to cooperate with neighbourhood people. Residents were outraged at the number of tickets they were getting for parking on the streets near their homes. They wanted to organize to obtain affordable permits for overnight parking. When the leader of our delegation presented our concerns and received the commissioner's promise to come to a community meeting, the people felt excited and empowered. This is one of my fondest memories from my days of community organization. The people felt, perhaps for the first time, that they had influence over their lives.

To be involved in this work was exciting, empowering, and fun, yet some questions remained unanswered. It seemed to me that the structures were not transformed but simply inverted. There were different people in power, but the disparity in how power was distributed remained. I had seen the "have nots" become the "haves." I saw people achieve the ability to act and their actions achieve solutions to the issues they had identified. Yet something was lacking. There seemed to be no corresponding interior change. There was an exchange of power yet no deeper change. I believed – hoped – that the power of domination could be transformed into an ability to act fully from within and among the entire Earth community. But how to bring this change about? Saul Alinsky said that there could be no true revolution (structural change) without an accompanying reformation (internal change). I understood the principle but was troubled when I saw active and vibrant communities later becoming racist and opposing the very things that had brought their organizing efforts into existence.

A classic example is the Back of the Yards project in Chicago's packinghouse district, the neighbourhood where Alinsky did his first major piece of work, bringing justice to the world of industrial workers. Today it is an embarrassingly racist community. This troubled me then; it troubles me now. The Back of the Yards project was a significant example of local democracy. People achieved political freedom in an industrial neighbourhood. Great things were accomplished as relationships were fostered and built. The organizing worked, but something went wrong.

True to Our Original Purpose

Relationship is the essence of existence.

—Thomas Berry, Brian Swimme

The predisposed tendency to engage in the paschal dynamics of life, death and rebirth is indelibly imprinted in our souls and operative in the unfolding processes of the cosmos.

Through conscious self-awareness we humans have the capacity and challenge to shape and form the culture in "trans-genetic" ways that can result in a world of harmony, balance and peace.

Whereas an ant that is genetically coded toward community will inevitably create an anthill, the human tendency toward community requires choice. Though we are genetically coded toward community, we have the responsibility to create the cultural forms that embody the tendency. For example, we have highrises and homes in gated communities, each an expression of the tendency for communion.

All cultural forms participate in the dynamics previously stated; they come into existence, they die (decline in their capacity to fulfill their purpose) and, it is hoped, are renewed and begin again.

The evidence of how cultural forms oppose their original purpose are starkly evident in everyday life; another politician lies, another student leaves high school still illiterate, another soldier dies in Iraq, another organization founded for good and noble goals opposes its original purpose.

An example mentioned here was Saul Alinsky's first major project, "The Back of the Yards," in Chicago's Slaughter House district.

As I reflect on these dynamics, I recall the wisdom that guided the farmers who made their living from the land near my rural Ontario home. To ensure an abundant harvest and to avoid the possibility of a reduced yield and a depleted earth, they ploughed under the field and began again.

To keep our work for justice alive and vital, we will need to renew, rework and reorganize our projects. Our goal will always be to ensure that our projects and programs remain true to their original purpose.

Despite having worked as an organizer in Southwest Chicago and the Riverdale and West Central communities of Toronto, there was still something missing. I was grateful for the legacy of Alinsky and his colleagues. I believed that the first act of justice-making is organization. I realized that organization is a way to get things done, a way of changing systems, and, I hoped, changing hearts. However, I was still searching for increased wisdom about justice-making.

While puzzling over these questions, I inaugurated a project called the Institute for Communities in Canada at Humber College in northwest Toronto. I invited to the institute a team of men and women who were at the time working with Paulo Freire and the Institute for Cultural Action. Freire, the Brazilian educator, had been exiled from Brazil and later from Chile for his educational methods. I thought perhaps his work would provide answers to my questions. His conviction that we need to liberate the oppressor as well as the oppressed – outlined in his book *The Pedagogy of the Oppressed* – was new to me; it changed my understanding of justice. I also began to see that trusting people is indispensable for revolutionary change. This insight collapsed the dualism implicit in a "have" *vs.* "have not" mentality.

Both Alinsky and Freire articulated a four-phase approach in their work. The phases converge in unexpected ways. Their manner is different, but their intention is very much the same. The following sections describe their approaches.

The Dynamics of Compassion

The silence of the stars is the silence of creation and recreation.

—Chet Raymo

Alinsky and Freire each begin with an initial stage of storytelling. They invite people to talk about their experiences and their hopes for a more just world. This initial storytelling provides the grounding. It assists people to envision their world in a different way. They clarify their vision as they hear what others have to say. The story gathers energy and provides an opportunity to experience unity. I was often told, "You organize with your ears." For Alinsky, this is the pre-organizing phase. For Freire, it is the descriptive phase.

The second phase focuses on the pain, obstacles, and structures that perpetuate injustice. This calls for dismantling systems that cause injustice. It involves shaking things up in order to form new patterns and relationships, new capacities to act. For Alinsky this is the disorganizing phase. For Freire, this second phase involves codification – naming the oppression through generative themes. He means identifying the internal obstacles and structural external blocks that take away internal freedom and the capacity to make external choices. For the people of Brazil, the external block was the military regime; for us today, it may be the policies of media, government, and corporations. The internal obstacle is fear.

The third phase is moving toward something new. For Alinsky, the organizing phase is about creating organizational forms for those who have no representation. Alinsky was fond of saying that "the organizer is driven by a desire to create." The organizer's work is to create organizations around issues for which there is no organizational response at present. For example, if a neighbourhood has small children and working mothers, an organization to provide day care may be needed. Another need may be an after-school program for children whose parents are still at work when they get out of school.

Freire also saw his work as a context for creativity. For him, education is the way we express creativity. It flows from us, teaches us, and ultimately transforms us. This is the phase of cultural action. He writes, "Education is an act of creation, capable of unleashing other creative acts, a process from the inside out."

Both Alinsky and Freire view their work as bringing things to a collective whole. For Alinsky, compassion and justice are accomplished through community organization by bringing the community together to develop a community of action. The old structures that are at the service of justice are combined with the newly organized ones. Together, they cooperate in the work of transformation.

The old and the new structures are woven together into a fabric for justice-making. This mass-based (involving the whole community) organization becomes the vehicle for resolving issues and working toward justice. This is the reorganizing phase. Whether expressed in a town hall meeting, a union gathering, or a political convention, something exciting happens when people gather to express their collective energy for justice.

Nature reveals to us that Earth is our sacred home, a place where balance and harmony exist. Communion and compassion, then, are both an awareness of interconnectedness (consciousness) and a determination to bring them about where they are not yet present. Communion and compassion heal the ruptures in creation by creating a bond that is intimate and full. Compassion is at the heart of the Christian tradition.

It is about relationships, love, celebration, and a reverence for Earth. Engaged cosmology will relieve our work of compassion from too much purpose and too many whys. It is about being, about participating in the divine creative energy that will heal Earth and render our planet whole. Our invitation is to experience compassion, to fall in love with our self, with one another, with Earth and the cosmos. In doing so, we become vulnerable, transparent, open, and connected.

To practice communion and compassion is to stop putting poison in our bodies or burying toxins in the ground. Communion and compassion call us to support ecological practices such as reforestation, which purifies the soil, air, and water. There is a direct relationship between our destiny and doing justice-making. Meister Eckhart wrote, "If you are to discover who you are, do justice." Compassion, the full engagement in life, provides a window of opportunity into the next step in our life. By engaging fully in the culture in order to change it, we achieve a new understanding and appreciation of the unity and the dynamic patterns that reveal its deeper meaning.

A Transformational Story

We explain things by telling their story – how they came into being and the changes that have taken place over time ... This is especially true in explaining those profound formative influences that have shaped our sense of the sacred.

—Thomas Berry

The journey into compassion is a journey into fashioning a new myth. Through myth we make sense out of what appears to be a senseless world. Myths give meaning to self and to community, tell us where we come from, where we are headed, and what is possible and appropriate. We need myths. We particularly need myths that support the transformation of the culture and connect this process to the dynamics of Earth.

The myth that is being born in our time is the way we understand our relationship to the planet. In 1948, world-renowned astronomer Sir Fred Hoyle wrote, "Once a photograph of Earth taken from the outside is available, a new idea that is as powerful as any in history will be let loose." We now have that photograph, and it is the seed of a new myth. By exploring the heavens we can achieve a new planetary ethic and a new *raison d'être* for the people of Earth. Community and compassion become our goals. War becomes even more untenable, and the liberation of all men and women is a mandate. The photograph of Earth from the outside has become a basis for healing separation and promoting our participation in a holistic universe, in an engaged cosmology. Saul Alinsky asserted that lifting despair is tantamount to "rubbing raw the sores of discontent."

For Alinsky, despair is linked to powerlessness and is healed when we are able to take possession of our lives. Paulo Freire described our experience as being programmed in a great computer where everything is predetermined and we have no control over our lives. In my view, despair is a result of blocked energy and unexpressed emotions. However, when people gather to act together and celebrate their accomplishments, something new and important happens: they feel more cheerful, empowered, and able to act in their own behalf. As a result, despair dissolves and hope emerges.

Places

Cascading hills
swirling turbulently
into emptiness
from a place of silent beauty
that proudly proclaims its presence
in a brokenhearted world.
Memories appear and
weave a tapestry of wisdom
calling out in the streets
to every galaxy and star.
Our moment is sacred.
It proclaims the God of all things
while we tremble at the threshold
of a doorway to the unknown.

Action Autobiography

An action autobiography is a great help in focusing energy and recognizing the patterns of your life and goals. I am including the following selections from my own action autobiography, written in question-and-answer format, as a template for others who would like to try this approach.

- *What is your earliest recollection of an action through which you tried to bring about change?*

When I was eleven, I made a deal with my baseball manager that during games that my brother pitched, I would catch. The other catcher on the team was older and better than I was, but my deal ensured that I would be able to play regularly.

- *How was this action a statement of hope and courage and confrontation with resignation and inertia?*

It took courage for me to try to change the system (that decreed the better player always would play) so I could obtain something that was important to me. It is also true that I felt somewhat ambivalent about my success, precisely because I was not the better player.

- *How did your action result in increased solidarity with others?*

My action increased my solidarity with my brother and with some of our teammates because it showed that we could influence some of the conditions under which we played.

- *Did this action increase your belief in people as a source of action on behalf of freedom, equality, and peace?*

While this action was my introduction to influencing power and creating change, I was still operating as an eleven-year-old child. From the perspective of values, my action left a lot to be desired in terms of freedom, fairness, and peace.

- *What people bring you hope, promote freedom, and model courage and compassion?*

There are many people who have supported my efforts and believed in me. Among them are Jack Egan, Thomas Merton, David Steindl-Rast, Thomas Berry, and my brother and sister. I would also include Dom Hélder Câmara, Dorothy Day and Pierre Teilhard de Chardin. There are also others, pastoral people of great faith and prophetic courage, who inspire me.

- Msgr. Jack Egan

I met Msgr. Jack Egan at the University of Notre Dame. As I sat in his office, the phone continued to ring. The people who called represented a cross-section of America's prophetic voices for justice.

Jack founded the Catholic Committee on Urban Ministry, on whose board I was privileged to serve as the Canadian liaison. He preached his gospel of "information, support, and the possibility of common action" to all who would join him in the work for justice.

One day in Toronto, when I was driving Msgr. Egan to the airport after his visit to support one of my projects, the Institute on Social Ministry at the Toronto Schools of Theology, he said, "Conlon, Canada needs a Jack Egan." Those words have lived with me over the years. His correspondence with bishops on my behalf and his timely notes and words of encouragement made it possible for me to create the free space necessary to continue my journey amid the turbulence and cultural earthquake of the post-Vatican II church.

The author and sociologist Fr. Andrew Greeley has called Msgr. Jack Egan the midwife of every significant Catholic Action movement in four decades. He was always ahead of his time and behind every issue. A consummate communicator, he believed in people and made it possible for those of us who were privileged to know him to believe in ourselves.

He is best described by his faithful colleague and longtime co-worker Peggy Roach, who wrote, "Father Jack Egan thought he could best serve God by serving all of God's people here in Chicago and across the globe. Their aspiration for justice became his agenda for a life of service. Today Jack would ask us: 'What are you doing for justice?'"

- Thomas Merton

Thomas Merton's writing has spoken to me since I first read *Seeds of Contemplation* during my seminary days. Today, every bookstore carries a selection of his books. Thomas Merton continues to speak to generations of seekers. From *The Seven Storey Mountain*, his best-selling autobiography, to *Inner Experience*, published posthumously, his books are replete with avenues of self-discovery and great significance for those who search and explore the depths of human experience, accompanied by humour, truth, and love.

When I visited Gethsemani Abbey in Bardstown, Kentucky, in the mid-1960s, I was unaware of Merton's significance; since his untimely death in 1968, his writings have been my constant companions.

- Dorothy Day

I never met Dorothy Day, although I tried. While still in the seminary, a friend and I traveled to Staten Island, New York, to visit her, only to discover that she was in Cuba! However, we did go to the Bowery in New York City, the home of the House of Hospitality of the Catholic Worker. There we saw her ideals of voluntary poverty and nonviolence at work. Today, these projects exist around the world. Together with Peter Maurin she founded *The Catholic Worker* newspaper, first published in 1933. Today, the Catholic Worker is still widely circulated, maintaining Day's commitment to nonviolence, the poor, and voluntary poverty. The following quotation speaks to the vision and commitment of this great woman:

What we would like to do is change the world—make it a little simpler for people to feed, clothe and shelter themselves as God intended them to do. And to a certain extent, by fighting for better conditions, by crying out increasingly for the rights of the workers, of the poor, of the destitute—the rights of the worthy and unworthy poor, in other words—we can to a certain extent change the world; we can work for the oasis, the little cell of joy and peace in a harried world.

- Dom Hélder Câmara

Dom Hélder Câmara from the diocese of Recife, Brazil, was internationally known as the Bishop of the Poor. Central to his work was the conviction that inhuman structures can be transformed through telling the truth and practicing justice. When I attended his talks in Toronto, sponsored by Ten Days for World Development, and later in Berkeley at Newman Hall, I felt that I was in the presence of a holy prophet. These words reveal the depth of his soul: "It is a pity there are people who will go through life never having thought of watching a sunrise."

- Brother David Steindl-Rast

Brother David Steindl-Rast, OSB, is to my mind the Thomas Merton of our time. His planetary consciousness, bridge building between East and West, and commitment to justice and peace are testimonies to his significance. His contributions are documented in his written works, including *Gratefulness, the Heart of Prayer*, *A Listening Heart*, and *Belonging in the Universe*, the last of which he co-authored with American physicist Fritjof Capra.

I hold my relationship with Brother David as a precious gift.

- *What do you want to create on behalf of Earth on the next phase of your journey?*

I would like to advance the work of geo-justice and engaged cosmology. I would like to contribute to the infusion of energy into the culture to build a spiritually-inspired movement to make possible the transition into a new era, a new time of reciprocity and mutual enhancement between humans and non-humans.

I would like to listen more, become more comfortable with questions than answers, and live out the wise advice of Meister Eckhart, "to live without a why."

I want to reflect on my life, honour and celebrate my mentors, many of whose names appear in these pages. I also want to contribute to a vibrant Earth community whose touchstone categories will be mutuality and reciprocity, a community that will see the signature of God in all creation, especially in the voiceless and most abused.

- *How have your efforts toward freedom deepened your experience of the divine?*

The words of medieval mystic Mechtild of Magdeburg provide much insight into this question. She wrote: "On the day of my spiritual awakening, I saw and knew that I saw God in all things, all things in God." I felt that her words confirmed my intuitive understanding. I felt I had come home to God, that I was as much in the divine as a fish is in water. I called this experience of being immersed in divinity being "at the edge of our longing" (the title of one of my previous books). I wrote of the longing of the soul as contemplative theology, longing of life as liberation theology, and longing of Earth as creation theology. I felt that viewing each of these longings through the lens of a theology and then weaving them together created a "spectrum theology." In a way, spectrum theology sees God in all things and offers a spiritual practice for the experience of the divine.

- *What have you seen, felt, or done to increase your efforts, and what do you intend to do?*

I read material related to my area of interest as much and as often as I can. I listen carefully to presentations, attend conferences, interact with students, and listen to new recorded resources.

I strive to stay in touch with my feelings, to be open to the pain of our endangered planet and its people; to understand and explore the courses and consequences of social injustice and ecological devastation without becoming obsessed with the challenges and, as a result, be less able to respond and be joyfully and hopefully engaged

I want to continue to study, pray, and act to contribute, as I am able, to the Great Work of nurturing a mutually enhancing Earth/human community.

- *What continues to hold you back?*

I am held back to the extent that I have internalized the unjust systems that oppress the planet and its peoples.

I am held back by fear, by lack of trust, by denying my deeper knowing, by lack of obedience to what I know is true, by failing to strive to achieve what sometimes seems like an impossible dream, by surrendering to the unlived life, by being unwilling to think "outside the box," and by fearing to go to the edge of my longing and do whatever needs to be done there.

- *In what ways have you worked toward unity between your awareness of the new cosmology and your actions in the world?*

In many ways my study, writing, teaching, organizing, and praxis have been a response to this and to the challenges posed in *From the Stars to the Street*. This book is an attempt to bring about a synthesis, a dynamic integration of my work in the world and the perspectives revealed in the new cosmology. My development of geo-justice and engaged cosmology focuses on a response to this question, that is, the relationship between the revelations available in the new cosmology and my actions in the world in behalf of Earth and its people.

- *What have you learned about yourself and about the earth through your engagement?*

The cosmological journey is an adventure in self-discovery. I have learned how the energy coursing through the universe can find direction and expression through me.

I have learned how the beauty of creation can elevate my spirit and nourish and heal my soul.

I have learned that my life is derived from the abundance available on this gorgeous planet.

I have learned that many of life's greatest treasures are transacted in silence.

I have learned that an integration of sacrament and covenant are significant components of strategic engagement.

I have learned that the new cosmology is a science of inspiration, joy, and hope, not a program.

I have learned that the new cosmology, however, is also the inspirational source of programs and that engaged cosmology is nourished by a new religious sensitivity – the energetic resources of the universe – and is itself the strategic result of the gifts available to us in the New Story.

I have learned that the New Story continues to reveal to us that awesome beauty, intense pain, and geo-justice are other words for God. Engaged cosmology is a way to name and integrate these initiatives.

I have learned to become aware, in these opening years of the twenty-first century, that we, as a people and as a planet, are at the threshold of something new. Inspired by the vision of a new cosmology, we are beginning to connect sacredness to engagement through video series, programs of integral transformation, and projects designed to make the New Story available to many more people. In ways similar to the approach outlined in these pages, a growing number of people, inspired by the awesomeness of the New Story, are drawing on mentors and "wisdom people" of the past and putting their insights to the service of all peoples and the planet.

- *How are you engaged with the forces of oppression and the symbols and sources of limitations in your life?*

I experience the forces of oppression in ecclesiastic, academic, and political structures. I have my personal struggles with fear, despair, and internalized oppression. In my confrontations I emerge with a heart often broken and a mind sometimes divided.

- *What has been your most prophetic effort on behalf of Earth?*

I think of the initiatives that have engaged people's efforts, that have been marked with continuity, and whose long-term impact is difficult to measure: a halfway house in London, Ontario, Canada; a centre for children, seniors, and the homeless in Sarnia, Ontario; a project for friends and associates of former mental patients in Toronto; a newspaper, *Catholic New Times*; the Institute for Christian Life; the Canadian Caucus for Theological Field Education; Regional Connectors in Creation Spirituality; Project Earth; the Ecozoic Council; Brothers of Earth; Sophia Center; and my books. I hope some among these efforts have brought about change and healing

- *What universal principles do you believe in and how do they serve to guide your work?*

I am increasingly aware that the ethics of the cosmos must guide my life. The principles of differentiation, interiority, and communion are central to my values. The wisdom of my Christian tradition and revelatory disclosures of my own story. The work for human rights and dignity is central to relationships, which in turn reflect the interconnectedness that is central to my life and future work. Together these principles form a trinitarian perspective that provides the framework for my life and work.

A Message from Micah

When the trees say nothing
St. Francis dances in the Sky

Sacred Words
Imprinted on my soul

I am grounded in the Journey
I encounter the divine

Clouds glisten
Telling many stories of a
Universe alive with love

And I wonder
What does Micah mean?

Why are "From the Stars to the Street"
Supplanted by your word

In this a salutation of wonder
Or an announcement of oppression and pain

And I ask again
What is the meaning of your words, Micah

Are you the voice of God
A messenger calling out for change

Help me to listen to your word
In this place where even the trees say nothing.

5

Wisdom

Wisdom deals with daily human experience in the good world created by God.

—Roland Murphy

My journey has consistently reminded me that there is discrepancy between what I declare to be true and how I live in the world. But the practice of critical reflection has made it possible for me to strive to narrow the gap between what I do and what I say. This challenge has been particularly evident in my relationship to the earth. In this regard I have been moved by recalling moments of encountering creation in my early years. Nourished by the beauty of the earth and the nature mysticism of the wisdom literature, I recall my first communions – those moments when my heart was moved by the encounter with creation and I experienced the Divine.

As Earth formed and our planet took shape, humans became a self-aware expression of life. The narrative quality of conscientization – critical reflection on our world for the sake of transformation – can be understood within the context of the story of the universe; it involves a process of "history making" whereby people become authors of their own destiny and responsible participants in the work of justice, transformation, and freedom. Thus education for critical consciousness will involve, instead of a teacher, a coordinator; instead of lectures, dialogue; instead of pupils, group partici-pants; instead of alienating syllabi, programs that are "broken down" and "codified" into learning units.

People in the streets, placards raised, proclaim injustice in the world. How are we to respond to "the great unraveling," the fragmentation awash in our lives, viscerally expressed in despair, anger, fear, and outraged actions? What strategies of change will make a better world for the children? Where do we discover a cosmic and cultural context for the work that lies ahead? In what ways can wonder and awe, beauty and brokenness, energize our ability to act?

Perhaps we can learn to listen with our hearts, feel the pulse of the people, and touch their souls. We then feel acutely the pain of our brokenhearted world but also celebrate with others the possibility of change. We dissolve fear with courage, despair with hope, obsession with awareness. With an ongoing interplay of action and reflection we move forward to transform the world. In and through our engagement we will learn to act in new ways that keep the universe in mind, new ways to think and pray cosmologically, to take up the challenge of this time both globally and locally.

> New ways to transform our world.
> New ways that are just.
> New ways that are strategic.
> New ways that are cosmic and cultural.
> New ways to listen.
> New ways to feel the pain of others, and of the earth.
> New ways to celebrate with courage, hope, awareness,
> and action.
> New ways to act with the universe in mind.
> New ways to respond with possibilities for engagement.
> New ways that are powerful, purposeful, strategic, and strong.

Cosmology: Earth Period

> *Humans give voice to their most exalted and terrible*
> *feelings only because they find themselves immersed*
> *in a universe filled with voices.*
>
> —*Thomas Berry And Brian Swimme*

God's speeches are a forceful rejection of a purely
anthropocentric view of creation. Not everything that
exists was made to be directly useful to human beings;
therefore they may not judge everything from
their point of view.

—Gustavo Gutiérrez

Adults often tell children, "Do as I say, not as I do." Each of us lives with a certain level of disparity between what we proclaim is true and how we live in the world. The goal of our lives is to create a greater congruence between our vision of how the world could be and our actions in the world. All of us live with a certain level of disharmony, yet we can strive to reduce the contradictions in our lives.

A First Communion

I remember the coming spring, robins in the yard, melting snow yielding rivulets of water. I remember the thunderstorms of summer, purifying the air and refreshing the land. I remember autumn in my Ontario home, when the large maple tree showered us with her leaves of orange, red, and green. I remember winter, with snow carpeting our village, and I hear again the silence being broken with the crash of ice floes on the stately St. Clair River. I remember the smell of freshly cut hay and wild strawberries in the field. I see fish jumping at dawn and recall the mystery of darkness as the sun sets on the banks of the St. Clair. I remember the sounds of silence echoing in my heart, the scriptures of creation inscribing my existence here on earth.

We gather in a cathedral of mountains, trees, and grass. Our choir is the crickets and the birds who sing on high. Our bread is a feast of beauty to feed the hungry soul. Our wine is the distilled wisdom of those who gather around. This Eucharist is gratitude for the gifts of life, and earth, an *ita missa est* to heal our broken world.

Culture: Popular Education

Conscientization contributes to bringing about the
kingdom of God; this is understood as total liberation
brought about by God's grace and power.

—Daniel Schiponi

Paulo Freire, whose work is one of the primary sources of the four-volume series *Training and Transformation*, had a great influence on my work.

I met Paulo Freire in Toronto in 1976 as a student in his seminar at the Ontario Institute in Studies in Education. It was a great moment for me and my classmates; we were in the presence of one of the most influential thinkers of the twentieth century. His great gift to the world, and to those of us who were privileged to be in the seminar, was his emphasis on dialogue and concern for the oppressed. His educational approach made it possible for each of us to realize that we were capable of contributing to the world and bringing about its radical transformation.

Wherever my journey has taken me, Paulo Freire's lessons on dialogue, the need for the importance of praxis (action and reflection), the power of conscientization (consciousness with the power to transform), and the capacity to honour lived experience have been my constant companions.

Once again I open my copy of Freire's book *Education for a Critical Consciousness*, with his fraternal good wishes inscribed on the opening page, and I am flooded with gratitude for having met this prophet of freedom whose life was marked by a commitment to the radical transformation of ordinary people. His works continue to have meaning for me today.

Freire was born in Brazil and started his career as a lawyer. With the realization that he was defending guilty people, he gave up law and became a philosopher and an adult educator. He was exiled from his own country and also from Chile. He ended up in Switzerland at the World Council of Churches in Geneva. As a result of his exile, his influence has spread around the world. I studied with Freire in the 1970s. I also studied at the Institute for Cultural Action with the coauthors of Freire's wonderful books about justice, spirituality, and popular education.

Paulo Freire worked with peasants in the Two-Thirds World, including Latin America, which was his initial constituency. He developed a process called *conscientization*, which is consciousness that has the power to transform the cultural reality. Paulo Freire, who died in the spring of 1997, was a prophet, a self-named "vagabond of the obvious." Freire did not think in either/or categories, but in both/and categories. Our culture often puts us in dualistic positions: If I go on retreat, I can't go on vacation. If I take this job, I will never get to the States. We put ourselves in boxes. But it doesn't have to be that way.

Following my encounter with Paulo Freire, I journeyed to the Gail Center in Cornwall-on-the-Hudson in New York State to participate in a popular education and community development event led by Sally Timmell and Ann Hope.

As colleagues and friends of Freire, they had just returned from working in Africa and were collaborating on what is now a four-book series, *Training in Transformation*, a guide for community workers. The most recent volume has a section entitled "The Life Support Systems of the Earth." One of our Sophia Center graduates, Hanna Remke, OP, was a major contributor to this section. I am awed by the interconnections of life!

As I have recounted, my journey toward geo-justice and engaged cosmology started with my parish work. Then I moved on to classical community development. Community development and community organizing in its classical historical sense are what Saul Alinsky learned from John L. Lewis, who was an organizer with the United Mine Workers. Alinsky took the organizing principles of the miners and applied them to urban neighbourhoods. Community development in its classical sense is like a business model – it uses methods and structures to solve mechanical issues in the community.

However, we are beginning to move beyond that model, and thus I came to the third step in my journey. One night I was at a Community Action Network meeting in Ireland, sitting with twenty-three other people. We talked about how soul work and community development are related. I came to see that soul work, the spiritual dimension of working within a community, is the creative side. The methodology for identifying the issue and who can solve it, of negotiating a change, is the industrial side of community development. Now we are in a transition stage in which we are building community, but not in a mechanistic sense.

I was asked once about the role that imagination plays in this process. I believe the following story illustrates it well. A friend of mine is a scientist in British Columbia. He told me about his teacher, who had written a very long problem, the solution to which required complex mathematical formulas. A young woman came up, looked at the problem, and instinctively knew the answer.

Community development is intuitive, the work of an artist. If people gather and examine the images that come from the recesses of their own souls, the collective imagination will flourish. What is going on in their community will be visible to everyone. Real community development in today's world is about bringing art into the community, whether it is music, visual art, poetry, or body movement. To evoke the imagination allows people to flourish.

Many people, like eleventh-century Hildegard of Bingen, heal themselves through art. (I believe that crayons and pencils offer one of the greatest cancer serums available to us.) To get the energy flowing in people's lives is the way to get a community to wake up, to be alive, but it is also a way to heal the whole person through evoking the issue, evoking the imagination.

In cultural action, people are invited to tell their stories and become subjects of their own destiny. They say, as a result, "Tomorrow, I will do my work with pride. I know that I am worthwhile." The result of the descriptive phase is generative themes. There are issues and concerns that emerge from listening to people and inviting them to name what is most on their minds.

As people tell their stories, they come to understand their oppression and the internal and structural obstacles that hold them back. A visual and verbal depiction of these themes is called a code. The code becomes a vehicle for critical reflection. In this process the people are able to increase their understanding of the issues and take appropriate action to heal and transform the world. To encourage reflection the following questions may be posed:

- What do you see? feel?

- What have you done? need to do? need to know?

- What do you plan to do?

The Shimmering Well

More than a lumber and stone,
more than a place to live,
more than a symbol of home
is the shimmering well by the sea.
More than a beautiful building,
more than a dream now come true,
more than a place to gather and talk
is the shimmering well by the sea.
More than a home for the restless,
more than a project for peace,
more than the soul's healing
is the shimmering well by the sea.
More than a place to be equal,

more than a place to be free,
more than a place for congruence
is the shimmering well by the sea.
More than a place to listen,
more than a place just to be,
more than a place for all creatures
is the shimmering well by the sea.
Yes, it's place for my story,
and a place of mystery for me,
a place of peace for all earthlings
is the shimmering well by the sea.

Questions

What lies within,
asking for a voice?
What lies within,
asking to be heard?
What lies deep within
responding to this moment?
What lies deep within
A voice from the heart of the universe
inviting us to respond to what
the earth is asking of us.

6

A Flowering of the Movement

Resurrection

I arise today
to the rustle of the breeze
to the pulsation of the planet
whose energy for life
shines Forth
in sight and sound.
I arise today
to the laughter of a child,
the smile of an elder,
the embrace of the Great Oak.
I arise today
amid news of death and darkness
that clouds our country's soul.

Prompted by a growing desire to create a dynamic integration of my experiences of therapy, community organization, popular education, global education, and the new cosmology, I developed the language and framework of geo-justice, a preferential option for Earth. This approach integrates the principles operative in the universe (differentiation, communion, and interiority) into cultural forms through local, global, and psycho-social components. The focus is to create harmony, balance, and peace on the planet and a palpable trinitarian presence of the Divine as manifest in Creator, Spirit, and Word. As religious educator Maria Harris says, "The demand is liberation, the emphasis is connectedness, the corrective is suffering, the power is imagination, and the vocation is the repair of the world."

Geo-justice – peace with the earth – implies a profound transformation of people and society. The work of geo-justice is a work of the heart, a falling in love with the divine voice that summons us to listen and become one with the oppressed. Passion and compassion for the earth and its people become a new vision that evokes fresh energy for the work of restoring devastation and relieving oppression. Through a preferential option for the earth we awaken to the needs of the planet and experience a new sense of hope, peace, purpose, and place. Our deepest longing finds fulfillment as the old order gives way to the new.

Geo-justice can be understood as a personal and planetary challenge to bring about personal, social, and ecological justice; it is a passionate and practical call to action that opens us to the beauty and the crises of our time. Geo-justice is about compassion, engagement, and participation. It evokes inspiration and hope as we contemplate a new era of novelty and surprise – a new creation that is about love, harmony, balance, and peace. Geo-justice is a cultural manifestation of the principles of the universe and a preferential option for Earth.

Another Word for Justice

The greatest beauty is organic wholeness, the wholes of life and things, the divine beauty of the universe.

—*Robinson Jeffers*

We sat together at Holy Names University in a staff meeting. Our purpose was to develop and name areas of concentration in the curriculum of culture and spirituality. We were looking for ways that our students could claim an area of study that would better equip them for the work ahead. One of the areas that we sought to name was in the area of justice and transformation. Within the context of the new cosmology our naming needed to be open to a cosmological perspective; it also needed to contain a meaning that continued the work of justice and change. The evening after our meeting I went to sleep and awoke with this word on my lips: *geo-justice*. When I reported it to our group and gained acceptance, a new source of energy flowed into my life.

I wrote my first book on the subject: *Geo-Justice: A Preferential Option for the Earth*. The word and the writings that followed became a context to bring together the elements of my previous journey. In naming the components of geo-justice I found a home combining community organization and con-scientization (local component), communications therapy (psychosocial), and my growing interest in a planetary perspective (global).

Geo-justice became a touchstone category for my work. Its naming was a watershed moment in my personal journey.

Paschal Mystery

The whole planet earth, as an entirety, must also be seen as a context for theology.

—*Tisa Balasuriya*

The dynamic of the paschal mystery (incarnation, crucifixion, and res-urrection) culminating in Pentecost is also the dynamic of our journey into justice-making. Thus geo-justice can be understood as a dramatic re-enact-ment of the paschal mystery (life, death, and return). As we awake from the dream of separateness, we understand more fully the revelatory dimensions of the story of the universe. Geo-justice views Earth as the body of God and the incarnational presence of the Cosmic Christ. It comprises the pattern that connects all dimensions of the community of life.

A New Cosmology

We must begin with an awareness that the explosion of modern scien-tific knowledge, which resulted in so much destruction, is now being assimilated into a new cosmology and a new wisdom.

—*Brian Swimme*

In the summer of 1983, in Toronto, I attended a workshop on creation spirituality. I was invited to do a sabbatical the following year at Holy Names University. I accepted that invitation, expecting to be there until Christmas. I am still here, because in California I was presented with a new understanding, a New Story.

This is a telling of that New Story: Once upon a time we took a whole bunch of helium, a whole bunch of hydrogen, put it in a big jar, and shook it up. Out came roses, cauliflowers, leprechauns, ethnic people, trees, and us.

That's the story. A little short, perhaps, but basically that's the story. This story changed everything for me. But how does it relate to our justice agenda? What does it have to contribute? As I reflected on my experiences in justice-making, many questions came to mind.

I now realize that it is one thing to work very intensely in a neighbourhood on the issues of drugs, education, homelessness, parking, immigrants and asylum seekers, housing, and so on. But it slowly became clear to me that one can't work on the streets in one area and not know what is happening on the planet. In other words, in Toronto, Seattle, or Prague, globalization has become a central issue of the cultural moment in which we are living. I couldn't work with people in my neighbourhood and ignore what was happening globally. Both local and global awareness are essential.

In 1977, two friends, Jerry and Patricia Mische, wrote a book called *Towards a Human World Order*. They were saying that one can't isolate a nation-state because it interacts with the whole planet. For example, the issues that are current in Ireland, whether with cocaine or education or travellers, are not just neighbourhood problems or even just Irish problems. They are global problems. Immigration is a global problem. In fact, every issue touches every other issue. They are all interconnected. If we are going to do justice, we have to have a global perspective. That is what I started to understand. I hadn't really grasped cosmology fully, but I knew that without a global perspective, my local efforts could be co-opted.

As my reflections in geo-justice deepened, I wrote in my journal: justice, peace with Earth, implies a transformation of people and society. The work of justice is a work of the heart – a falling in love with the divine voice that summons us to listen and become one with passion and compassion for the oppressed Earth. Our challenge is to integrate all of this, that is to say, the cosmology and the call of justice. We are people of two paradigms with shifting cosmologies, changing stories, striving to heal the separateness between the spirit and the street, the crack in the ozone layer and crack cocaine, vision and despair, the wounded heart and a planet both beautiful and in pain. Brother David Steindl-Rast has said, "Global mysticism is a number one anchor for solidarity." In other words, we are at one with the planet when we are at one with one another. Remember the picture that was taken in 1969 from outer space, looking back at Earth – this jewel hanging in space? All the astronauts who went into that space capsule as soldiers came back as mystics, because they saw this view for the first time.

I have seen well-intentioned people's lives sacrificed on the altars of community work, cases where community development actually became instrumental in the disintegration of families. One woman, a mother, said, "It is a stretch to be involved in community." What does it mean to be stretched? I've seen people become very involved in their work and eventually become emotionally fragmented. It is always a danger.

Organizers have to deal with the psyche as well as the social dimension of life. If we don't nourish our soul, the community is not going to be a place where real justice happens. If we do injustice to our own psyches, how can we be just to others? I have proposed that we should have both a counselor and a community development person in every project, so that the people's lives, as well as the structures of oppression, can be dealt with. I call this the psycho-social dimension. Freire talks about an "inner dynamic." Dom Hélder said, "The greatest struggle of our time is to integrate the inner life and outer life." One of the dangers in the community development process is becoming so focused in the external that we forget about the internal process.

In justice work there must be a local component grounded in the neighbourhood and bio-region. It is one thing to feel strongly about the global issues and take them on. It is another thing to deal with the inner and outer life and the health of the local community that is involved in doing the work. And there are also worthy local issues. We used to describe the local and immediate as "where the rubber hits the road." This is the local component of geo-justice. Geo-justice at that point in my journey was connecting these three components – global, local, and psycho-social – and viewing them through a cultural lens.

My prayer was this:

Where there are ruptures in creation, we are aroused to peace.
Where there is disquietude, we are invited to balance.
Where there is discord, we are attuned to resonance.
In and through the pain of our wounded planet we are
called to make our Easter with the earth.
From collapse and devastation we rediscover within
the risen heart of the universe,
cosmic peace,
profound harmony,
deep balance,

compassionate resonance,
Pentecost for the earth,
and geo-justice for the universe.

I received a note from the co-founder and president of Global Education Associates, Patricia Mische. "The three components that you have developed for geo-justice," she wrote, "correspond to the three principles that come out of the universe story." I developed these principles and their cultural implications for geo-justice more fully in *Earth Story, Sacred Story.*

Another person who helped me clarify my commitment to these principles is cultural historian Thomas Berry who has had a profound influence on my life.

When I first met Thomas Berry, CP, at Holy Names University, I was unaware of the profound impact he would have on my future work. These powerful, poetic words from "Morningside Cathedral" capture his passion for the earth:

> What sound
> What song
> What cry appropriate
> What cry can bring a healing.
> ~~~~~~~~
> Lamenting our present destiny
> Beseeching humankind
> To bring back the sun
> To let the flowers bloom in the meadow.
> The rivers run through the hills
> And let the earth
> And all its living creatures
> Live their
> Wild,
> Fierce,
> Serene
> And abundant life.

Over the intervening years I have come to know Thomas as a man of great intellect and immense compassion. I, like so many others, have felt encouraged and supported by him. He was born in the hills of North Carolina, and was ordained as a member of the Passionist Community. A scholar of cultural history, he dedicated his life to the study of the dynamics of the universe. He calls himself a geologian, that is, a theologian of the earth. His writings, in particular *The Dream of the Earth, The Great Work*, and *Evening Reflections*, have articulated a vision that has ignited great interest. Many projects around the world that are working to bring about a more viable Earth community, including our work at Sophia Center, owe a debt of gratitude to Thomas Berry, whose vision is a testimony to the grandeur and splendor of each place, and the beauty of each moment.

These principles, embedded in all of life, have been articulated by others, including Thomas Berry and Pierre Teilhard de Chardin. The first principle is that everything is related to everything else: *communion*. Science tells us of the "butterfly effect," that minute changes in New Zealand – the flap of butterfly's wing – can affect the weather pattern in Ireland. We are planetary citizens, interrelated with all things and with the universe itself. In other words, relationship is the essence of existence. That is the global component of geo-justice. If we are going to do justice or be justice people, it needs to be within the context of the planetary relationship.

And what does the cosmological word *communion* mean in the world of justice? The spiritual or theological equivalent is the *Pentecost path*. It shifts how we understand justice and compassion. Social justice can sometimes be elitist, when, for example, there is an imbalance in the relationship.

The whole notion of service is totally revolutionized when we understand that union and compassion come out of how the universe is organized. It is about equality. It is about the mystical connection we have to the poor. Gustavo Gutiérrez, the father of liberation theology, wrote that "God is more present with the poor not because they are better but just because they are poor."

There is a powerful presence of the Divine in the vulnerability of those who are poor. In 1946, Pius XII published the encyclical *Mystici Corporis* (The Mystical Body of Christ). My conviction is that the mystical body of Christ is a metaphor for the planet Earth; we need to apply liberation theology's language of a preferential option for the poor to the planet. Canadian theologian Gregory Baum writes, "If we don't look at our lives through the lens of the poor, we will blame them."

I remember being in Mexico one time with a young Canadian exchange student. We were driving through Mexico City and saw the *barrios* around the city. The young man claimed that the people were living in these shacks because they were lazy. A preferential option perspective would see things differently.

The preferential option for Earth includes Earth's people. All people. Earth is the metaphor and the context of our lives. Every authentic spirituality or theology is contextual. Liberation theology is contextual. Every country, every context, has its own spirituality. Spirituality out of context is fundamentalism; it has a tendency to be applied without awareness of where we are. Unless we take the context into consideration, our actions may be misguided and inappropriate. The religious right in the United States, for example, is vulnerable to this critique.

Everything in the universe is related, but nothing is the same. A tree has leaves, but no two are the same. God is not repetitive. Thomas Aquinas said, "The only thing that God cannot create is God." God cannot repeat God, but anything else is possible. So, everything that is created is some dimension, some reflection, some aspect of the Divine. Differentiation means no two grains of sand, no two trees, no two people, no two snowflakes are identical. Think of the marvel of that. In Canada, as a child, I used to look for two identical snowflakes a lot. And I am still looking. But the principle of differentiation tells me I'm not likely to find them.

Central to justice is the ability to embrace difference. Let me give you an example. Why do we have racism? We have racism because we resist seeing that somebody who is different from us is yet another reflection of the Divine. Why do we have sexism? Why do we have religious persecution? The answer is the same. Justice is about the celebration of differentiation. Injustice is about the denial of difference. The celebration of difference is the most profound act of justice that we can demonstrate and sometimes the most difficult.

The second law of thermodynamics means that there is energy in all of us, in all the universe, to create. The act of differentiation is an act of creativity. Without differentiation, each act is simply repetition. If we go into a community development project with the answers before we even listen to the people, we're repeating what we know. This is not creativity.

The writings of medieval mystic Meister Eckhart have spoken to me at a very profound level since I was introduced to his work more than two decades ago. The words of this great Christian mystic and Dominican priest remain current today and are relevant to themes of this book. Eckhart writes:

If you know what I have to say about justice, you know everything
I have to say. If you want to discover who you are, do justice.

Eckhart's theology of divinization focuses on the "divine spark" that
remains alive in each person and all aspects of creation, especially in the
poor.

Meister Eckhart was perhaps the most influential Christian figure of the
Middle Ages. The popularity of his writings today can be attributed to his
focus on the sacredness of life and the call to live a joyful, compassionate,
and deeply human life.

He writes, "If your heart is troubled, you are not yet a mother. You are
still on the way to giving birth." Creativity is the closest we can get to God.
Eckhart continues, "God lies on her maternity bed all day giving birth." The
theological word for creativity is *resurrection*; it means something is emerging
through us. The creative act pulls through us, whether the result is a picture,
a poem, a conversation, or a community meeting.

It wrestles with us. It is completely consuming. but it is also both sat-
isfying and liberating. Justice is born from the imagination. *Differentiation*
is the cosmological language and *resurrection* is the theological or spiritual
language for creativity. Geo-justice does not deny the human, but neither
does it limit itself to the human. Social justice is a dimension of geo-justice,
but the two are not equivalent. Geo-justice is Earth justice. It involves the
rain forest as well as the unfed child.

Teilhard de Chardin said we have to spend more time with creation
than with redemption, that the human story is a dimension of the universe
story, and that everything has a psycho-spiritual dimension. Think of how
important that is for the ecological movement. No longer can we say, "Let's
take that animal to the lab and experiment with it. It's just an animal, after
all." Or, "Let's cut down the trees. They are there for our use." Or, "It's all
right to oppress people of that race. After all, we are better than they are."

Once a blind man visited the Grand Canyon in Arizona. His friends
were looking around and noticing all the people, the tourists, the airplane
going over – everything but the view. The blind man was listening to the
tour guide and leaning over the guardrail into the canyon. Finally he nudged
his friend, pointed, and said, "Isn't it beautiful?" He couldn't see a thing. But
he experienced it. He had the Grand Canyon inside him. Just as we do. He
had that interior life. There is a Grand Canyon in us just as big as the one
in the American Southwest. That is interiority. A dimension of interiority

also resides in a cat or a tree. If we could awaken to this dimension, which is present in all life, then we wouldn't talk about the earth as dirt, or cut trees without listening to their pain. The mystery of interiority awakens us to a psycho-spiritual dimension.

I now realize that there is a soul dimension within geo-justice. In order to do justice we need to realize, first of all, that we are in communion with all of life. Then we need to see that there is a task for us to do, one that calls forth our creativity and totally respects and celebrates difference. This task is uniquely our own. As Saint Francis of Assisi reminds us, "I have done what is mine to do. May Christ teach you what is yours to do."

Leonard Bernstein was an influential conductor and composer; he played an important role in the development of American music. In his controversial *Mass*, the celebrant stands in the chancel holding a crystal chalice. He throws it onto the marble floor, and it shatters into countless pieces. As he looks at the shattered pieces of crystal on the floor, he says, "I never thought that brokenness could be so beautiful." This event is a symbolic fall of the ideals of the 1960s as articulated in the song "Things Get Broken."

If we see that the poor are like pieces of a broken yet beautiful chalice on the floor of life, then we can see the uniqueness that shines through every one. We are more than we seem. We are stronger than we think we are. We are deeper than we understand. In a way Leonard Bernstein's *Mass* epitomizes both our culture's recent history and the enduring aspiration for a better future that resides in every heart.

Rainer Maria Rilke names a mystical cosmology when he writes:

> God speaks to each of us only in making us
> And then walks silently with us out of the night.
> But the words before our beginning,
> cloudy words, are these:
>
> "Sent out by your senses,
> Go to the edge of your longing,
> Give me something to wear.
>
> Flare up like a fire behind all things;
> So that their shadows expand
> to always cover me fully.

> Let everything happen to you: Beauty and terror.
> Just keep going: No feeling is the farthest out.
> Do not let yourself be parted from me.
> Near is the land
> which they call life.
>
> You will know it
> by its earnestness.
>
> Give me your hand."

—Translation by Br. David Steindl-Rast, OSB

There is that intense longing in all of us. I feel it more these days; maybe it's because I'm not as young as I used to be. There is also this interior search, a hunger for intimacy and contemplation, the hunger that Thomas Merton knew when he wrote that "the life of every man is a mystery of solitude and communion." None of us resolves this question easily. To have relationship and depth is to go to the edge of our longing. I believe this is precisely what the geo-justice process is about. The paschal mystery is not only a divine event; it is also the action of the Earth and its people.

Pulitzer Prize winner Gary Snyder is a major literary figure of the twentieth century, presently teaching literature and wilderness thought at the University of California at Davis. His poetry reaches into the recesses of our souls and challenges us to participate in the restoration of the natural places from which many feel estranged. He is a voice speaking for the non-human and the value of the wild and the sacred. He expresses it this way:

> I pledge allegiance to the soul of Turtle Island
> One ecosystem
> In diversity
> Under the Sun
> With joyful interdependence for all.

As members of the earth community, we stand at a crossroads. Sixty-five million years ago, dinosaurs, for reasons still unclear, became extinct. Their passing marked the close of an era. Today, another planetary era is coming to an end, but for reasons that are far more clear. A vast devastation is being unleashed on Earth: species are dying, water is unfit to drink, oceans are being destroyed, soil is eroding, oil slicks and burning oil wells wreak havoc on ecosystems, bridges are collapsing and roads deteriorating, and more and more children are abandoned to live on the streets of our cities. Meanwhile, the primary structures of our world community – our nation-states, corporations, churches, and schools – contribute to oppression and death rather than liberation and life. This time of crisis and transition cries out for geo-justice.

Geo-justice calls us to discover the converging terrain of personal, social, and environmental justice. It calls us to passionate and practical action that makes us aware not only of the crisis of our times but also of the primal beauty of our Earth. We are challenged to liberate Earth and its peoples. We are called to practice geo-justice.

The Emergence of Geo-Justice

Without mysticism politics soon becomes cruel and barbaric; without political love mysticism becomes sentimental and uncommitted interiority.
—*Edward Schillebeeckx*

We are beginning to awaken from our cultural trance and perceive the pain of Earth and its peoples. We are approaching a watershed moment, the beginning of a cosmological shift in Earth's history. With this shift comes the need for a new way of seeing and a new way of acting. The implications and proportions of this task are enormous. Cultural indicators, such as the removal of the Berlin Wall and the 200 million people who participated in Earth Day 1990, are signs of far-reaching historical and social change. We also see signs of denial in this time of transition. For example, while it is clear that our dependency on oil must end, we still go to war over it. We must choose the direction we want to go. The words of scripture have compelling relevance to the situation at the beginning of the twenty-first century: "Today, I call heaven and earth to witness against you: I am offering you life or death, blessing or curse. Choose life, then, so that you and your descendants may live" (Deuteronomy 30:19).

This crisis demands that we discover new ways to live out our vocational destiny, new ways to become participants in the harmony, balance, and peace that Earth can achieve. We need new ways of becoming instruments of an Earth-centered compassion. Just as iron filings are drawn by a magnet or as individual flames coalesce into a larger fire, we are approaching a crystallization of consciousness. We are getting closer and closer to a collective awareness that supports and expands mutually enhancing relationships with Earth. Geo-justice is a preferential option for Earth.

Geo-justice can be seen as the paschal mystery that locates itself within Earth. The cross is the death of the world's tropical rain forests, the struggle of starving people in Ethiopia, the tragedy of HIV/AIDS, the erosion of our cultural soul from drug abuse. The surprise of resurrection, inexorably connected to the cross, is found in the rhythm of ocean waves, the caress of an evening breeze, the rich promise of a plowed field, the coming of spring, the touch of a loved one, the joy for a newborn child, the impulse for human rights, and in efforts toward ecological balance.

In geo-justice, we journey from the empty tomb of cultural collapse and a devastated Earth into a new era of surprise and continuity marked by a new people and a new Earth. This new creation will be more about love than laws, more about harmony than competition. It will be nourished by listening to Earth and being open to the creative process emerging from the whole Earth community.

Geo-justice is always a work of the heart, more about compassion, engagement, and participation than about reaction, obligation, and separateness. Geo-justice brings about inspiration and hope as we awaken to the sacred dimensions of the earth community. It invites our participation in the fabric of compassion woven within Earth. In it we see our future and well-being intimately connected to the well-being of the planet.

Cosmic Crucifixion: Dying as a Transforming Act

We hear within our hearts the sound of earth crying.

—*Thich Nhat Hanh*

In our time, when this dazzling array of life we call Earth is fast becoming a wasteland, we are invited to be hospice workers and to sit at the bedside of dying institutions. Geo-justice demands that we let these old structures go and create something new that is allied to the dynamics of bringing new life to the planet. Resuscitating dying institutions is futile. Rather, we need to put our vital energies where there is the potential for life and not more death.

As winter follows autumn, we must face the hard death of old ways created by the petrochemical era. For example, we need to pollute less by creating an alternate means of transportation. We must bring about new structures, new stories, and new forms, while we let go of the hysteria of consumption, our well-learned response to advertising which has become an addictive behaviour.

Experience tells us that illness can be a source of transformation, a doorway to new life. Cancer is the runaway reproduction of specific cells that divert needed nourishment from other, healthy cells. Our culture suffers from a cancer that drains the world's resources away from life-giving work in order to nourish an uncontrolled proliferation of weapons and waste.

AIDS, a truly terrifying illness that erodes the immune system, is pandemic in our time. Yet people with AIDS are often sources of hope and revelatory of life's deeper meaning. A person with AIDS captured this reality in saying, "Avoid the virus but expose yourself to AIDS." Correspondingly, Earth today is afflicted with a weakened immune system brought on by pollution, pesticides, abuse, and neglect.

As we plunge into the dark night of our cultural soul, we come to terms with the grief of the planet and become open to the dazzling images of new life emerging among us. From the perspective of geo-justice we see that the cosmic crucifixion can lead us to wellsprings of hope, if we bring new vision to this critical moment of collapse and devastation. Death can be the doorway to new life, an avenue toward vitally needed transformation.

Making Our Easter with Earth

Resurrection happens with an awareness of the cosmos when we celebrate our personal and collective capacity to heal the fragmentation within and alienation from without.

If the cosmic crucifixion is to lead us to new life and transformation, we must die to our alienation from Earth and to a dualistic world view that separates women from men, rich from poor, people from other aspects of creation. We must die to addictive patterns of living that substitute products for people and capital for the dignity of labour. When I met Paulo Freire, he described his work as an educator as "making my Easter." For him, to engage in education was to die and be resurrected. This archetypal metaphor for the paschal mystery is an appropriate one for the work of geo-justice, for Earth is both crucified and restored to new life.

Making our Easter with Earth is also about dying to the absolute authority of our governments and public leaders, whether they are in Washington, Ottawa, London, or Tokyo. We need to listen to the radical collective wisdom emerging from reflections taking place in church basements, living rooms, and community gatherings. Dying institutions cannot lead us into the future. Rather, new visions and new forms must be generated from the narrative that unfolds when communities talk together about their relationship to one another and to the land.

Although it is about sacrifice, geo-justice is not about obligation and denial. It is holistic – fully connected to and grounded in Earth. Geo-justice is not an anthropocentric alternative to true healing; it is an approach to liberating Earth and its peoples.

Geo-justice weaves together the global, local, and psycho-social. For example, as mentioned, the rubber workers in the Amazon rain forests first became concerned about the forests because their livelihood was at stake – a local concern. Gradually they joined forces with the global effort to save a resource precious to all the world – a global dimension. In the process they developed a keener understanding of their own potential and power – a psycho-social dimension. Thus, each component affects and is affected by the others. Making our Easter with Earth, then, is about working with these three components as we search for new language and life-affirming images for our common work.

Seeing that we are one with Earth is the starting point of geo-justice. This experience of communion with the planet is necessary for global solidarity and peace. This awareness of Earth as one has erupted into human consciousness.

In the words of Thomas Merton, we have "awakened from the dream of separateness." One of the great treasures the astronauts brought back from the moon was the image of our blue-green, living Earth as seen through the window of their spacecraft: the image. Without global unity or oneness, our experience on Earth will continue to be one of divisions of nations, of gender, of class, of race, of haves and have-nots. When we awaken from this illusion of separateness, however, we become architects of a truly new world order. We celebrate our oneness with Earth as we take up the challenge to think of the cosmos while acting both globally and locally.

Geo-justice is about being fully present to the sacred space in which we live. It was because of where they lived that the rubber workers of the rain forests became connected to one of the primary life systems of Earth. We tell our personal stories of Earth locally, where the needs of the people are heard. When we remember our relationship to the land, we make a psychic pilgrimage that connects us with the earth as a sacred place.

When we weave together a tapestry of relationships to celebrate our connection to Earth, we are propelled into prophetic action. We come to understand Earth's oppression as our own. We see our interior life linked with the entire universe – the mystery within as great as the mystery without.

Historically, justice workers have fallen into an either/or mentality. In most programs of preparation for service (ministry, social work, and so on), personal development is seen as a precondition for action. Yet, as a community organizer, I witnessed the destruction of marriages, the fracturing of relationships, and the erosion of personal health in the name of what was best for the community. Alternatively, I have seen people go into therapy and lose sight of the importance of politics and structures as a basis for change. For some people, outrage about injustice is more about their personal problems than systems of oppression.

Geo-justice challenges us to embrace our interior life and the world around us as one – to heal the fragmentation within as we confront our alienation from Earth. To connect our personal pain to the pain of the cosmos requires awareness. We need to access the healing properties of the psyche and increase our compassion for Earth through vision and actions that are unifying and holistic. The concept of geo-justice offers a dream in which we will work together to build a better world by following a vision of beauty, love, laughter, and peace. The geo-justice vision is giving birth to a new consensus among people with diverse histories, denominations, languages, and cultures. The process moves people toward a holistic world view and a meta-religious spirituality. We need to develop a cosmological imagination to bring about this paradigmatic shift. This transformation is already taking place, and is of enormous magnitude. It gives birth to informal networks of information, support, and possible common action. Through these networks, we are developing new ways of seeing and acting in the world.

Emergence of a Planetary Pentecost

Jesus's prophetic commitment set out to form a movement of renewal;
the new community was a place of equality and inclusivity. There was
to be no coercion, no violence directed to anyone inside or outside the
community.

—Dennis Edwards

For Christians, Pentecost marks that moment, fifty days after Easter, when the Holy Spirit descended on the people and gave birth to the Church. As a result, all of humanity was offered the possibility of friendship and participation in the paschal mystery, the dynamic of life, death, and resurrection that is the centerpiece of our Christian journey. Planetary Pentecost is a truly inclusive vision of a community that embraces the entire world and every species. It allows us to experience great hope and shared responsibility for all creation. A Planetary Pentecost happens

- when we experience relationship and interconnectedness with all creation;
- when each member of the Earth community experiences and expresses reciprocity and peace;
- when all creation becomes a manifestation of sacredness and grace; and
- when the divine creative energy of creation erupts in our psyches and infuses the landscape of our soul.

It is the energy of interconnectedness within the psyche and our political and social systems; it is a descent into a greater understanding of the inter-relatedness of all life. It weaves together a fabric of relationships that heals what is broken, reunites what is separated, and recreates the face of Earth.

At the end of World War II, singer Vera Lynn made popular a song called "When the Lights Go On Again All Over the World." It was an anthem of peace for our planet, a reminder of how the world becomes interrelated "when the lights go on," when people could leave their lights on without fear that they would become the target of bombers. When I was a child, I was always amazed when, walking down the streets of my hometown in Ontario at dusk, the streetlights would suddenly come on. In some way it helped me understand the meaning of Lynn's song and the meaning of Pentecost. For me, light and fire have always meant healing from the powers of darkness, separation, and alienation.

Planetary Pentecost is a work of the heart. It is our response to the voice that summons us to heal the pain of Earth and its peoples. We listen to this voice by being in touch with our own pain and connecting it to Earth's pain. As in deep ecology, we see no distinction between ourselves and Earth; we see that we are one. When we respond with this mindset, fragmentation and alienation are healed.

The phrase *cosmic ache* speaks to me of the profound and abiding connection we have with Earth. The ache draws us and activates in us a sacred impulse to respond. Our response contributes to a planetary Pentecost; we discover that good things are happening, and we strive to make the world better. We become a new people, a new creation in a transformed Earth.

A planetary Pentecost is hopeful, prophetic, empowering, and practical; it frees us from helplessness and despair. Growing out of the story of the universe, it is a celebration of this revelatory moment. It reminds us that justice in and through Earth flows naturally from the processes of life.

At the heart of geo-justice is the realization that we are as much of the earth as the rocks, the water, and the trees. The work of geo-justice – its implication for transportation, housing, corporations, schools, churches, cities, states, nations, the land, and our own lifestyles – is our work for today and our hope for a better tomorrow.

A Possible Future

In giving their lives they find life
In serving others they lose the fear that crippled freedom
In reaching for the best in every person,
that make each of us more free.
In respecting the life of every man and woman,
They make life more precious for us all.

—*Cesar Chavez*

More and more, people are awakening to their responsibility for healing the wounds of our Earth. In all parts of the planet, individuals and groups are coming together to share a common vision. They give one another support and provide the information needed to bring harmony and balance to life systems and cultural relationships. People are converging to create a possible future. They have discovered a language, a process, an operative myth for balance and harmony on the planet: they have discovered geo-justice.

There are many wonderful and effective projects for justice-making and social change on our planet. Justice in and through the earth is a work of the heart – a falling in love with the divine voice that summons us to become one with the beautiful and oppressed Earth.

The rhythms of life, death and resurrection are central to the dynamics of creation. Indeed, the Jesus story continues to unfold. Bethlehem is present in our lives, and the cosmic crucifixion names the human ecological death present to us each day. Every day, we make our Easter with the earth and celebrate the emergence of Planetary Pentecost in our midst. My reflections on geo-justice have grounded me in this struggle and continue to provide a context for reflection as I contemplate the mystery of my own life's journey. I struggle to express the fruit of my reflection.

Dying

Dying for a cause
for empire
for oil
for "freedom"
for "God"
Dying for a vision
of children
of new life
of hope
of trust
of peace
of possibilities

Show Me

Show me life
With fullness of expression
Flowers bursting
Birth everywhere
The universe on fire
Saying poems to the sky

Show me life
Replete with expectation
Sound of praise
Proclamations of,
Goodness
Joy, and
Wonder

Yes, show me life
Full of nooks and crannies
Edges sharp and smooth
Show me life

Show me brokenness
In pain, and joy
And solemn celebration
Oh yes, show me life
Amplified expression, of
Birth and Death

Doorways and thresholds
Always open
Sonnets of joy
Songs of apprehension

Yes, please show me
Take me to the precipice
Of every possibility
And set me free
For life

7

Solidarity and Wonder

What liberation theologians are saying today, and many others too, must be involved (engagé, as the French say).

—Albert Nolan

Engaged cosmology's address is at the intersection of wisdom inscribed in the universe, tradition as recorded in Scripture and the biographies of our time.

In "in-between" times such as the present, there is an uneasiness across country after country. The news is full of destruction and fear hovers in the air like a gathering storm poised to release devastation on trembling earth. Yet, somehow, new life begins to emerge. Genetic memories begin to activate Earth's collective soul. Newfound webs of friendship begin to grow, and beauty appears amid brokenness. Wisdom begins to proclaim new hope from the treetops of our land.

Humanity invents itself. Love burns incandescently in the hearts and minds of everyone who courageously proclaims an affirmation of new life. Hope happens. Beauty shines forth from the ashes of the former day. We experience delight and discover who we are. The universe visits our hearts, and the cosmos comes home to our street. Life is made new; joy happens; sadness makes us strong; enduring effort is its own reward.

A fresh urge to act pulses in our veins. What we know in our hearts makes our spirit strong. Narratives of engagement culminate in enduring acts of peace. As all our stories – cosmic, spiritual, and personal – weave the narrative of our life, we discover a fresh capacity to heal. With hearts made strong and a world more vital than before, we venture forth to discover strength in our fragility, health in our pain, vitality in apparent death, and newfound faith in what we somehow always knew was true.

Humanity and all creation speak out and celebrate; each voice is a proclamation of divinity and the source of all creation. We align our energies with the unfolding dynamics of the universe, and the incarnational presence of the cosmic Christ is manifest, a presence that is suffused with wisdom, awareness, justice, harmony, balance, and peace. The kingdom of God on Earth is the culminating act of engaged cosmology through reading the signs of the times, participating in social analysis, creating an operative cosmology.

Through acts of organization, popular education, and personal and cultural healing we are able to bring the kingdom now, with justice to a world in pain.

A Continuing Personal Quest

Each belonging moves us toward a new longing and a new belonging.
—David Steindl-Rast, OSM

On my own quest, with many of my earlier dreams now dashed by the reactionary storms of repressive leadership and vertical hierarchies seeming everywhere, I continued my search. I attended a summer institute on race and the cosmos, followed by a conference and institute on engaged cosmology.

Along with others, I began to seek ways to take what we had learned over the years and place it within the context of the new cosmology. From this perspective the challenge was – and still remains – to find approaches to heal our brokenhearted world and bring hope and renewed possibilities to the youngest and most vulnerable occupants of our planetary home.

And so my journey continues. Engaged cosmology has become not only my passion but a compass for my journey. These pages are yet another chapter on the way. It is my enduring hope that with others I can continue to work, study, pray, celebrate, and question as our lives unfold together until we see a beacon of hope on the horizon, shining more brightly than before, an indicator of justice that will guide our lives and bring about a better tomorrow for everyone.

This Cosmological Moment

Today we are able to take yet another step toward our shared destiny, deep liberation and profound fulfillment.

—Brian Swimme

Engaged cosmology is a contextual view of the world from the perspective of the universe, our faith tradition, and the concrete cultural conditions of humanity on earth. It views both the awe and wonder of the night sky and solidarity in acts of protest and prophecy as one act that makes it possible for beauty to shine through as an expression of balance, harmony and peace.

Engaged cosmology is energized by a theology of contemplation, liberation, and creation and an integration of the Great Story – the story of the universe – and the story of our faith tradition as revealed in Genesis, Exodus, the Prophets, the paschal mystery, and the reign of God.

Engaged cosmology names our participation in personal, social, and ecological transformation (personal healing, organization, popular education, and geo-justice). The Holy Spirit is the Bible's way of explaining the power and presence of God within the life of the community, within the lives of individuals, and within the whole of creation.

The Spirit is the inner source of energy, movement, and life; it is also the promise of the future and the source of new birth and new creation. The Spirit promises that instead of destruction there will be a new Pentecost, a new heaven, and a new earth.

> When the day of Pentecost had come … suddenly from heaven there came a sound like the rush of a violent wind…. Divided tongues, as of fire, appeared among them…. Your sons and your daughters shall prophesy, and your young men shall see visions, and your old men shall dream dreams. (Acts 2:2-3, 17)

The Divine Presence in Our Unfolding Story

> *The universe presents itself full of mystery and meaning … the basic norms of human activities can be discovered from within the profoundly spiritual process that is the universe itself.*
>
> —*Thomas Berry*

As the earth formed, our planet home took shape. Human beings expressed life with self-awareness and the capacity to reflect on the universe and the earth. Each voice – human and non-human – is a proclamation of divinity. By aligning our energies with the unfolding universe, humanity participates in making divinity present in our lives. We experience the incarnational presence of the Cosmic Christ, a presence that is suffused with wisdom, awareness, justice, harmony, balance, and peace.

As I contemplate such a world, I feel inspired by the gospel mandate to contribute to bringing about the kingdom of God in our midst. I visualize a time when we enable beauty to shine forth, speak truth to power, comprehend the powers of the universe, and support the stories of our faith tradition. Perhaps then engaged cosmology will emerge in our midst, and the reign of God will be palpable and present. As Thomas Berry reminds us, "The basic norms of human activities can be discovered from within the profoundly spiritual process that is the universe itself."

Tradition: Reign of God

The intoxication of advancing the kingdom in every domain of humanity.
—*Teilhard de Chardin*

The kingdom of God on Earth is a culminating act of engaged cosmology. It offers a radical hope of justice for all, especially the poor and most abused of God's people and creation. Jesuit Jon Sobrino goes to the heart of the issue: "God is more interested in justice than in sacred rites. God is more in tune with the cry of the oppressed than with the praises of the pious. Actions are what count, not homilies."

Prayer for Engaged Cosmology

Let me be an instrument of engaged cosmology.
Where there is emotional turmoil, grant me clarity.
Where there are structures of oppression,
grant me the ability to act.
Where there is conviction that the dangers either don't exist
or are too great,
grant me critical reflection.
Where there is glum plodding and tired abstract justice,
grant me the fresh energy of geo-justice.
Grant that I may be able to transform upset into moral outrage,
systemic oppression into strategies for change,
hopelessness into celebration.

Engaged cosmology creates a synthesis of empowerment from a cosmic and cultural perspective. It draws on the insights and energy of theology,

111

psychology, sociology, organization, popular education, and cosmology to create a world of justice, a world for a better tomorrow.

Culture: Engaged Cosmology

If you give your bread to the hungry, and relief to the oppressed ...
you shall be like a watered garden, like a spring of water whose waters
never run dry.

—Book of Isaiah

Engaged cosmology is both vehicle and vision to heal our broken world. It provides a context within which to work, study, pray, celebrate, and question. Engaged cosmology can become the new narrative of the West, revising and revitalizing our traditions and our culture.

Our continuing quest is to discover how to embrace the mystery of the universe and integrate our spirituality with our actions. As we seek to advance our work in the world, we are faced with several challenges.

The first challenge is to make the new cosmology more accessible to different professions and social groups. We need to awaken people to the insanity of the day and help them become aware of those things that are most essential in our diminished world. We need to point out that most of the dominant media are vested not in the transmission of news but in spreading the propaganda of their corporate owners. To counteract this we need to support alternative sources and enable them to gain access to a wider audience. A few examples are *National Catholic Reporter*, *Sojourners*, *Air America*, and *Catholic New Times*.

Part of the challenge is to make the new cosmology more accessible through heightened consciousness. We need to increase our level of commitment to finding ways to change as we dip into the cosmic energy and creativity that are available to us.

Faith, Spirituality, and the New Cosmology

The universe is a single, vast, celebratory event. Here the poetry, the
music, the mystique of the Earth all find expression ... We are able
once again to hear the music and experience the depth of fulfillment that
are available to us, once we are attuned to the symphony around us.

—Thomas Berry

Our different religious and faith traditions are confronted with sorting out a variety of questions. Among these are images of God and integrating faith with the New Story. Religion and ecology publications are a major source for discussion about these questions. We need strategic approaches based on the new cosmology that are tempered with social analysis. We must communicate the power of a vision that is mythic and profound. Only then will it be possible to listen, to be receptive, to see suffering as a dimension of the journey we are taking in company with God and all creation.

We are asked to describe the practice of social justice and eco-activism so that they can be understood as seamless and interrelated. The combined practice of social justice and the new cosmology requires a prolonged engagement, a desire and willingness to go deeper into the issues of our time; it calls us to uncovering the dynamics of relationship; it seizes the imagination and moves us into action. The environmental justice movement can be viewed as a model; the global justice movement can be viewed as a context in which ecological and social justice are connected in relationship to the issues of race, poverty, and war. Popular education can be an effective approach to dealing with these issues.

The new cosmology relates to the healing of the human and the experience of psychology, mysticism ego, and activism; it has an impact on personal and social behaviour. It is important to be grounded in the story and to transcend any tendency toward despair and alienation.

We need to appeal to the idealism of youth and to offer young people a vision to ground their lives in the new cosmology in order to increase their resistance to a world of uncertainty, consumerism, and narcissism. We need to avoid empty or false optimism and provide real hope through stories of change and transformation.

Our spirituality will be strengthened and enhanced when we link religious communities with ecologically-based local projects where community can be fostered and experienced. In those communities we move beyond fear and experience the impact of powerful archetypal symbols of connectedness (the New Story). In this way we will overcome both insecurity and the dangers of fundamentalism. Through the formation of small faith-based communities we will be healed of alienation and insecurity.

It is essential for us to see that ecology and environmental activism are not separate from what we are learning about the universe. How I live in my place on the planet and view this within the larger context of the universe is the enduring challenge.

Strategic Responses to Our Challenges

No revolutionary movement is complete without its poetic expression.
—James Conolly

Every decision matters. We need to awaken to the magnitude of the challenges before us. We need to become poets and politicians engaged in intensive dialogue with the signs of the times as we engage in the principles, strategies, and tactics appropriate for the practice of cosmology. As we ponder our strategies we ask:

- What challenges are most urgent?
- In what areas are we called to move forward now?
- How can we engage the people in the "mainstream" culture?
- What will happen when we take the new cosmology seriously?
- Is there a specific impasse we now face?
- How do we negotiate between the micro and the macro levels?

Engaged cosmology brings hope to a humanity wounded by a prevailing culture of dominance and oppression. It provides a language and an approach that connects cosmology to our traditions and energizes mediating structures in the culture to initiate new actions that are positive and transformative. Engaged cosmology is the child of imagination and courage; it is inscribed in our lives and in the constellations of the universe. It is an expression of our ongoing quest for fulfillment. It is nurtured by constant effort and unwavering trust in people and in the cosmos.

The Wind

In a seasonal swirl
bright sunshine lights up
a snowbound world
radiant with new light.
Breezes abound
sweeping forth the day
and once again reminding me
of the mystery of tomorrow.
Memories from the past

ripple the curtains
and provide tantalizing glimpses
of what lies ahead.

Engaged Cosmology

The kingdom of God will come as a civilization of
poverty, in opposition to the civilization of wealth.

—*Jon Sobrino*

Our cosmological moment is a one-time opportunity. Just as the galaxies formed when the conditions were right, so also are we present at a new moment when the universe is breaking through in new forms. What is happening in the universe can also happen through us: the ideas and projects we long to bring into existence will truly be realized.

Our hopes are nourished by the realization that

- Cosmology can advance through its interactions with this cultural moment and the social sciences (psychology, sociology, economics, politics).

- Other constellations and groups (such as environmental groups) are also asking questions about how to build a movement.

- There is an increasing recognition of the importance of values, religion, and spirituality in society (for example, the Preamble of *The Earth Charter* speaks of an emerging universe).

- There is an increasing emphasis on peace, justice, and human rights issues. Leadership in these important areas is essential. The new cosmology can become the master narrative.

In general, then, we can say that the planet and the human community long for a functional cosmology. The challenge is to communicate the new cosmology, and that means creating a language that is both accessible and true to the wisdom of the story. Participating in reflection groups provides opportunities both to think ourselves into new ways of acting and to act ourselves into new ways of thinking.

As we explore the "fault lines" of our psyches, we will become whole through the integration of contemplation and action experienced as the seamless garment of engaged cosmology.

Through in-depth reflection on the new cosmology we strive to ensure that our actions will flow from and be empowered by the wisdom of the universe itself and result in an ecologically healthy civilization. Through this process we will continue to explore new initiatives in light of the New Story. This approach will ensure the deepening of our understanding of the new cosmology and its potential as a resource for strategic action, action that responds thoughtfully to the challenges that lie ahead.

Enhancing the Great Work through Engaged Cosmology

The joys and the hopes, the griefs and anxieties of the people of this age, especially those who are poor or in any way afflicted, there too are the joys and hopes, the griefs and anxieties of the followers of Christ.
                                                                                    —Gaudium et Spes

Engaged cosmology is an expression of universal solidarity. From this perspective there is no outsider, no "other," whether human (race, creed, country, gender, and so forth) or non-human. All are associated with the divine creative energy and the deep wisdom of the universe. Being grounded in the experience of home is an essential precondition for the work of engaged cosmology.

Sadly, we recognize that many people have to overcome unhappy childhood experiences to reach the positive concept of home we are speaking of here. The concept of a nurturing home nourishes our sense of self. It names where we come from and where we are going. Home develops within us an experience of love, security, society, politics, and economics. Home reminds us of joy, tenderness, kindness, and what it means to live in the universe. In a time of war, terrorism, and escalating violence, we increasingly feel the need come home to ourselves, to our friends, and to the planet.

The metaphor of home provides us with the opportunity to explore the points where the engaged self meets the larger questions. Art, for example, is an area of engagement that can move us forward. Art captures the imagination and provides a framework for communication energized by music, dance, drama, visuals, and word. The arts speak to people's hearts. Artists are the visionaries of cultural movements; they tap the powers of the universe and invite us to become co-creators of the next phase of the story, cosmic companions in the struggle for justice.

Education is another area of importance. When we introduce small groups of people to the New Story, we do so in response to the problems and concerns of their lives as they express them. They become energized to participate in the work of transformation on personal, social, and ecological levels through critical reflection on the challenges present in their lives in light of the New Story.

Because at present there are few programs that offer education in the new cosmology, we need to support one another and begin to envision an institution that would house and teach the best of this New Story. There is a need for teacher training in the new cosmology; properly prepared, teachers will be empowered to move hearts, invite others to find their voice, and help them find an audience in the larger community.

Popular education is foundational to engaged cosmology. It comprises generosity, compassion, political awareness, ethical conduct, gestures of hope, and a contagious love of life all focused on creatures, both human and non-human, and on Earth itself. Currently, a group of people from various countries and cultures is preparing an initiative to make available key principles of engaged cosmology to a wide number of participants, particularly those living in the fourth world (developing countries). The goal is to develop a process that is experiential, shareable and accessible. The project is called "Crossing Points of Wisdom – Popular Embodiment."

We are invited to delve into the issues of our time through prolonged engagement that begins with vision, expresses itself in action, and is nourished by spiritual practice. Social justice and ecology are connected and call for an integrated response.

We need to increase our understanding of the new cosmology and to build a solid intellectual foundation. On that base we can nurture an incarnation of the new cosmology that will enrich our dialogue and ensure the integrity of our actions. As we study, learn, think, and create we will, little by little, unlock the wisdom of the universe.

Critical reflection and action will enable us to move away from the unquestioning acceptance of the current culture by corporate media and to support and develop alternative media and education for the task of transforming consciousness. We will become more comfortable with change. Our work will be energized and nourished by deep listening that connects us to our own passions and our contributions to the Great Work.

Emergence of Engaged Cosmology

One world is dying, another waiting to be born.

—*Matthew Arnold*

As the universe and society arrive at a new moment, something new is happening in our midst. Spiritual seekers from all traditions are forming networks of information and support. A new synthesis of the universe story, the narrative of our sacred texts, and the biographies of actions in the world is taking place. Engaged cosmology is coming into being.

At this point of engagement we will discover new resources for the journey, resources that find expression in generosity, sacrifice, reciprocity, relationship, and creativity.

As we take action that is congruent with the wisdom of the universe and our traditions, we are moved by the power of the cosmos and the legacy of commitment that flows from our tradition. We are energized by interdependence, liberation, and an ongoing celebration of awe, wonder, and oneness as we participate in engaged cosmology; vision, action and spiritual practice form a bridge into the new era that awaits us.

We awaken to a new and significant paragraph in the Great Story unfolding among us, especially in places on the planet that are neglected and oppressed. As those places are transformed in beauty, we feel keenly the connection between the wisdom of the universe, the promise of our traditions, and the dynamic capacities that pulsate through our lives.

Engaged cosmology is a process that is both ancient and new, cosmic and cultural. It is a defining moment when each of us is called to compose a song of engagement – a hymn of creation – turning the page on a new chapter for humanity and of all creation. Thus a song of hope for the future emerges, a tapestry of friendship and imagination.

A new community dances around the tree of life, whose roots are planted deep in the earth. The tree's trunk gives expression to a fully functioning democracy and economic system that is sustainable and diverse, while its branches reach out to embrace all those who long for a preferential option for the Earth. Through the practice of engaged cosmology we will bring hope for the children, unite the stars with the streets, and become fully committed to healing a brokenhearted world.

"God writes the Gospel not in the Bible alone, but on trees, flowers, clouds and stars."

—*Martin Luther King Jr.*

Nature's Challenge

Torrents of nature's outrage
ravage the shores of existence,
collapsing the separateness
between the poor and the possessor.
Newness erupts
as the tides subside,
once more bringing into balance
the foundation of our lives.
Life blossoms
in the springtime of our souls
and once again
peace reigns on God's green earth.

~~~~~~~~~~~~~~~~~

Deep wells
of cosmic wisdom
emanate
from the recesses of the soul.
Galaxies of beauty
create a resonating tone
and sing forth the conditions
through which compassion can shine.

8

Our New Freedom –
Wonder, Beauty and Belonging

A bird does not sing because it has an answer.
It sings because it has a song.

—*Chinese Proverb*

When asked when civilization was born, anthropologist Margaret Mead replied, "When the first femur was healed." She continued, "When the people were surrounded with enough compassion to allow the healing to take place."

This is a timely statement in a world whose brokenness is so palpably present in the challenges confronting major institutions, the life systems of the planet, and the spirit of our peoples.

Our task is to evoke the recuperative powers that will heal society and our endangered Earth. Fresh energy and a zest for existence can revive our spirit and heal the fragmentation and brokenness so palpable in our midst.

There is a story about a blind lady who often takes public transportation. Despite her lack of sight, this woman has the psychic sensitivity to perceive the presence of other passengers and, because of this capacity, seldom sits in a seat that is already occupied. However, sometimes she does. She thinks this happens only when that person's energy is so fractured that she is unable to detect his or her presence.

This absence of vital energy occurs not only in the occasional individual but also in many public institutions that have strayed from their original purpose and now stand in opposition to the gestures of generosity necessary for people to fulfill their destiny and realize their life purpose.

Yet there is hope. It seems to me that humanity is regaining its access to the recuperative powers of the universe. A new religious sensitivity is appearing in the soul of people whose energies are aroused by the beauty of creation and who have an increased awareness of the voiceless and the most abused. The universe, the wisdom of our Christian tradition, and the stories of our communities are converging. We are coming to believe that new ways are possible and that healing can happen in our world. We realize that healing is possible because of a profound spiritual change. Despite humanity's incessant search for healing through extended therapy and medical approaches, both traditional and natural, there has remained a deep-seated conviction that our efforts will fail. Our search for healing has been self-defeating because on some profound level we have been taught that we *cannot* be healed. The conviction that we are fatally flawed finds its origins in a theology that has spent more time on redemption than creation, more time on sin than celebration, and more time on healing than being healed itself.

As this barrier is removed, the divine creative energy available in the cosmos and operative through our faith traditions is increasingly available. As we discover greater access to these recuperative powers, healing becomes possible. As we approach the threshold of a new civilization for Earth and every creature, brokenness shimmers with beauty and our hearts and planet Earth hold out the promise of becoming whole again.

This approach involves weaving a membrane of energy to envelop our brokenhearted world. It demands moments of honouring and supporting self-healing. Rather than being agents of healing, our task is to get out of the way, providing only support and removing the obstacles that stand in the way of wholeness. Then healing happens, beauty shines forth, and each of us and all that is will become whole again.

Perhaps then the awe and wonder of the universe, the wordless wisdom spoken so eloquently by the rising sun at dawn, the rustle of the trees in a summer breeze, the cry of a coyote in the meadow, and the gurgle of an icy brook in winter will heal the broken heart of the child living with AIDS, the river burdened with pesticides and petrochemical waste, the rain forest crying out in anguish as its body is devoured.

Perhaps then all people will hear the prophetic voice of Sr. Dorothy Stang as her body received the loggers' bullets that took her life, or see Fr. Pierre Teilhard de Chardin's vision of the divine milieu. Yes, perhaps then we will begin again to see ourselves as walking stars, people of wonder and prophecy engaged in a cosmic journey, a healing adventure that will unite beauty and brokenness and bring about a great healing. The practice of en-gaged cosmology will create a seamless garment of justice and bring together the stars and the streets. Then we will heal a world devastated by tsunamis of grief and greed, poverty and pollution. Then beauty will come back to the earth and the stars will illuminate our streets.

Health is vibrant participation with the creative energy of the universe.
—Brian Swimme

Healing Our Story

The nature and scope of the conceptual crisis facing psychology and psychiatry is comparable to the situation introduced at the beginning of the twentieth century into physics.

–Stan Grof

Psychology has evolved a great deal since my early days in therapy. In those years psychoanalysis was the overarching framework. Its primary ap-proach was to review, remember, and re-experience the past and thus become freed of the emotional forces that held us captive and curtailed our ability to act in a healthy and authentic way.

My experience in therapy reflected the practices of the times (late 1960s and the 1970s), although it was in many ways more advanced. One of the things I learned in therapy is that the body, as well as the mind, is a reservoir of feeling and unexpressed emotion. A response to this insight resulted in my participation in a process called bioenergetics, described by its founder Alexander Lowen as "a therapeutic technique to help a person get back together with his body and to help him enjoy, to the fullest degree possible, the life of the body."

Alexander Lowen's work in bioenergetics created an avenue to the spiri-tual with such works as *In Tune with the Infinite* by Ralph Waldo Tine, and honoured the collective unconscious through group-oriented dream work and work therapy (participation in organic gardening, carpentry, and construction projects under supervision within the context of group therapy).

At the same time we were immersed in the Newtonian-Cartesian paradigm; psychology and religion/ spirituality, although coexisting in each of us, seemed literally worlds apart. Although not adhered to, the cultural tenet that the Divine was a projection to be healed and eradicated from our consciousness by sufficient therapy hovered in our midst. Lifestyle goals were conformed to the dominant culture, and a well-integrated social conscience combined with a passion for personal healing seemed absent.

When I moved to the Bay area in California, an encounter with Stan and Christina Grof at the Spiritual Emergence Network, then housed at Esalen in the Big Sur area of California's central coast, shifted my understanding in a profound way.

Through the Grofs's consciousness research (involving deep breathing, evocative music, body work, and mandala drawing) much was accomplished to advance the work of personal healing and its implications for a peaceful planet. Not only did the Grofs revolutionize the understanding of psychotherapy, but they have made significant strides in revealing how psychology can contribute more profoundly to a sustainable society and peaceful planet.

Psychology and modern consciousness research combined to become a powerful and sacred resource and a vehicle for healing our brokenhearted world. Stan Grof says:

Deep reverence for life and ecological awareness are among the most frequent consequences of the psycho-spiritual transformation. It is my belief that a movement in the direction of a fuller awareness of our conscious minds will vastly increase our chances for planetary survival.

When we pursue an inquiry beyond certain depth, we step out of the field of psychological categories and enter the sphere of ultimate mysteries of life. The floorboards of the soul, to which we try to penetrate, fan open and reveal the starry firmament.

—Bruno Schulz

The Ability to Act

Never do for people what they can do for themselves.

—Saul Alinsky

From the seminal thinking of Saul David Alinsky and his Back of the Yards project in Chicago's slaughterhouse district, the practice and principles of community organizing have endured through the last half of the twentieth century and remain vital today.

123

Community organizing has continued to unfold, from neighbourhood meetings around community issues, such as The Woodlawn Organization (TWO) in Chicago's South Side black community, to the Citizens' Action Program (CAP) that swept across the entire city. As Ed Chambers, director of the Industrial Areas Foundation (the project founded by Alinsky) asserts, "There is no substitute for fire."

That fire ignited the interest and energies of the poor and middle class across North America and beyond. That fire infused ecumenical partnerships and congregational participation among interest groups related to race, class, and gender. Through the political process, community organizing has given people a share in power proportionate to their importance for the welfare and survival of the whole community.

As Saul Alinsky sees it, community organization is a means to move the world as it is to the world as we would like it to be. The community organizing projects that have emerged over the years now are embodied in a network that transcends grassroots politics and geography and has become a "community of communicators," people whose close friendships and shared power have enhanced their capacity for meaning and contributed to a shared destiny filled with hope, joy, and equality.

As community organizing has evolved, it has connected the roots of the issues and the ability to act with the values that reside in people's commitment to their tradition. Grassroots activist Ed Chambers writes, "When people act on the gospel values and hold one another accountable, you've got a revolutionary act." When this revolutionary act is nourished by the language of scripture and tradition, a palpable experience of the presence of the Divine is possible.

For example, the Old Testament story of the Exodus tells of the forging of a people despite hardship, despair, and the apparent impossibility of their situation. In *Cold Anger*, Mary Beth Rodgers argues that a direct link between belief and community action exists. Affirmations and actions could be viewed as an outgrowth of a gospel concern for the poor, while simultaneously enriching people's lives and enhancing their experience of community in a significant way.

Reinventing Culture – Rereading Our Universe

Human consciousness comes into the world as a flaming ball of imagination.

—Maria Montessori

Popular education is extending its transformative influence to heal and hold sacred our people and our precious planet.

Paulo Freire is one of the greatest educators of all time. His many writings are read around the world and are foundational for the work of engaged cosmology and other initiatives that are designed to create a better world for every species. His approach has inspired educators, theologians, activists, and artists around the world. His work reflects his generosity, compassion, political awareness, ethical conduct, hope, and contagious love of life.

Freire's work is a challenge to our cultural moment and to injustice everywhere; he worked for the liberation of all people so that everyone could become a subject of the transformation of society. Like many prophets, his life was marked by significant cultural moments during his lifetime – humanity's voyage to the moon, the women's movement, liberation struggles around the world, technological developments, political upheavals, and above all, popular education movements.

Ann Hope and Sally Timmell have recently written a fourth volume to complement their original *Training and Transformation*. In their new work they have extended their focus to the Earth. Once again we witness popular education extending its transformative influence to heal and hold sacred our people and our precious planet.

The process of involving people in the transformation of their own reality is as relevant as ever. As they move forward in their work, they consistently respond to the needs of the elements – earth, water, fire, and air – the basic support systems of the planet around which revolve concerns about gender, race, culture, and poverty.

As in other approaches to transformation and change, popular education works to build a movement to activate and support networks of people in local communities.

A Preferential Option for Earth

Today we use terms like geo-justice to describe the essential connection between the personal and the ecological, the spiritual and the earthly aspects of our call to be justice makers.

—Diarmuid O'Murchu

125

The work of geo-justice starts as an act of self-discovery. As Meister Eckhart writes, "If you want to discover who you are, do justice." Geo-justice is also the foundation and basis for authentic relationships. Through the processes of self-discovery and right relationships, we are challenged to develop an analogical imagination, taking what we have learned in our new cosmology and applying it on personal and social levels.

Geo-justice is a response to and a language for the interrelationship of personal justice, social justice, and ecological justice. The story of the universe and the story of personal, social, and ecological justice are dynamically integrated through geo-justice. Geo-justice reminds us that we are located in the universe and connected to a vast constellation of relationships that are both singular and unique. It tells us that we are members of the family of life as well as the human family.

Geo-justice will result in a culture that is organic, differentiated, feminine and masculine, communitarian, and always open to change. Geo-justice, understood in this way, will support those aspects of creation that are spontaneous, cosmic, and connected, and that promote an understanding of humanity as related to the whole of life.

On its deepest level, geo-justice is more about being than doing, a listening spirituality that sees Earth and every species as a source of story and divine communication. It is a planetary spirituality of engagement and application that joins the universe and a personal, social, and ecological culture. It's about living in the question rather than fixating on predetermined results. It teaches us to listen, because, as Rosemary Radford Ruether states, "There is another voice, one that speaks from the intimate heart of matter that beckons us into communion."

The Dawn of Engagement

That star leads each one of us differently, one way or the other in accordance with our vocation ... The star for which the world is waiting, yet without yet being able to give it a name, or rightly appreciate its true transcendence, or even recognize the most spiritual and divine of its rays ... all we have to do is let the very heart of the earth beat within us.

—Teilhard de Chardin

We live in a brokenhearted world. It is a time when the military/petroleum complex is churning because of decreasing amounts of oil and water (blue gold, now polluted and scarce) upon which this culture is built; a time when global warming is real, no longer a research project to be administrated by government; a time when increasing numbers of species are vanishing; a time of deaths caused by poverty and diseases like HIV/AIDS; a time of terrorist attacks in a world awash in war.

But we also live in a time when something new and encouraging is happening. Like the Free Speech Movement, which was born on campuses and gatherings decades ago, something new is begging to arrive on the shore of this new day. It is a time when hearts are being lifted and bridges are being built between science and theology, between action and spiritual experience. There is a growing awareness of relationship and the reality of interdependence, a greater realization that an authentic life is a function of reciprocity and a keen desire to belong.

As we experience radical amazement at the wonder of the universe and extend compassionate action to the poor and suffering, the least, the lost and left behind, we awaken to a new opportunity. Our response will be prompted by an enhanced sensitivity that extends to self, other, Earth, and God. It will be signified by widening compassion as we respond to the needs and desires of all members of our planetary community.

Through contemplation, liberation, and creation-centered engagements, we will witness the unlocked power of each person, connect the stars to the streets, and inaugurate the work of engaged cosmology.

In this new historical moment we confront injustice and discover a new meaning of grace through the experience and practice of fairness, fulfillment, freedom, community, and unconditional love. Our experience of grace will offer fresh understanding of each benevolent moment and each person whose unconditional love permeates all of life and all creation.

The capacity to transcend social isolation and patterns of separation will increase the experience of acceptance and belonging. It will move us to appreciation and solidarity, supported by gestures of deep listening and recognition. In our spiritual practice we will discover a new sense of community and fulfillment, a new experience of mutuality, love, and increased capacity for vulnerability.

The experience of support, newfound friendships, and belonging will strengthen our work and provide increased purpose and meaning to our lives. From this new place we will collectively build an agenda for the future that is energized and practiced within a web of genuine engagement expressed as a balance of vision and action. Our new engagement will heal the degradation of abusive power while it inspires courage, creativity, and hope; in circles of solidarity we can imagine a better future and, as civil rights activist/historian W. E. B. Dubois phrased it, "respond to the mighty causes that call us."

Through the practice of engaged cosmology we participate in acts of service and justice at an unprecedented level; our engagements bring out the best in us and connect our actions to our hearts. We realize that what needs to be healed is our sense of separation. We locate ourselves within this universe and discover a world of love, kindness, and caring that transforms fear and despair into trust and hope.

Through the practice and appreciation of contemplation, liberation, and creation we establish an integral and inclusive presence that is open to the Divine and committed to a life of service and compassion. Increased trust and solidarity will heal and transform our cynicism and turn boredom into radical amazement and a life of engagement and spiritual practice.

Each person's narrative of engagement will embrace faith and be transformed in a new world of love and social solidarity. People of engaged cosmology, uniting the stars to the streets, will address the concrete circumstances of life with expanded consciousness and a new sense of the sacred, viewing everyone as a member of a beloved community nourished by a fresh and universal and inclusive spirituality. We discover the strength to "put feet into prayer" and move forward with inspiration and a new energy.

We listen to the echoes of the liberating mantra "Let my people go" and move from being victims to liberation. We are energized to build a new Noah's ark – a cultural context constructed by acts of hope, service, and justice. A new politics of peace will culminate in a revelatory moment that invites us to stand in awe of the universe and ourselves, to embrace the possibilities, and to make an enduring commitment to tomorrow.

The new ark will be a place to travel together into a promising and fruitful future; a place where truth and affection will nurture a world enveloped in peace and goodwill; a place with a growing awareness that we are not alone; a place where hope will carry us forward into a counterculture marked by non-cooperation with the consumer-oriented mainstream culture. We will experience homecoming in a silent revolution inspired by Francis of Assisi, who proclaimed, "Preach the gospel at all times. If necessary, use words."

Jean Vanier is one of Canada's great spiritual leaders. The son of a former Governor General, Vanier is known for creating an international organization of faith-based communities designed to provide homes with people who have developmental disabilities. Vanier's work, L'Arche, is certainly an example of building a new Noah's ark for our time. Recognition of the ability to accept and form community with people who have developmental disabilities is fundamental to his work.

L'Arche was begun in France and now has over one hundred projects in Canada, Australia, and the United States. Vanier's great compassion for people with handicaps has taught us many lessons. Each of us is wounded in some way, although some wounds are more visible than others. His gentle strength has resonated around the world.

I remember occasions when he would come to Toronto to make a presentation. The atmosphere was serene and spiritual. When he spoke to the late priest and author Henri Nouwen, and said, "Henri, you have come home," he was speaking to that wounded and homeless part of each of us. He was offering us passage on the new Noah's ark so needed in our brokenhearted world.

My friend Laura Pieke, when involved in a field placement with children with learning disabilities, wrote the following words: "I learned that people with learning disabilities are remarkable. Even though they might have difficulty grasping some aspect of things, they focus on their passions and let these take them away to a land all their own, occupied by no one but them and their dreams. I learned that they have wonderful things they love to do – it is pure magic."

Laura's appreciation for the "wounded ones" echoes the vision of Jean Vanier; she, like so many others, is a builder of the New Noah's Ark.

In the dawn of engagement a new awareness will shine through, a new relationship of interdependence and creativity, a new understanding of consciousness operating in the universe and empowered by the metaphors of belonging, mutuality, and the dynamic of putting love into action. These forms of engagement will be revealed in patterns of reverence and gratitude that will connect our actions to the heart; actions of contemplation, creativity, community, and celebration; actions punctuated by healthy intervals of rest and enjoyment.

The dawn of engagement will flourish when we create a "container," a context where we can give our gift in a community designated as a place that dissolves fear and where values, actions, and our highest aspirations can be expressed. It will be a place to dissolve old patterns of complicity that have resulted in a society that continues to produce more and more goods that are available only to those who need them least.

The practice of engaged cosmology will involve self-discovery and the exploration of identity. It will include coming home to a rootedness in our spiritual tradition enhanced by the various wisdom sources; it will heal alienation and support a profound integration of inner work and meaningful actions taken up to heal the people and the planet.

The Great Work of engaged cosmology will heal the distance modern technology often constructs between ourselves and those we are called to serve and encounter. Separation prevents us from interacting and communicating, and plunges us into the experience of a culture that fosters efficiency over empathy, competition over cooperation, and individualism over relationship. It is a culture that tolerates religion without transcendence, art without beauty, education without character, and law without justice.

The Great Work and the practice of engaged cosmology call us to reinvent our humanity, to explore the space within our psyche, to discover the oneness that unites us to all. Then we will be able to heal this dark moment, turn back the threat of apocalypse portrayed in the terrifying icons of mushroom cloud, collapsing towers, and security alerts.

As we replace fear with love and brokenheartedness with relationship and intimate presence, we see again, like the astronauts, a whole and healthy planet, the Earth seen from outer space.

The Great Work of engaged cosmology requires an intimate moral presence based on a profound respect for each member of Earth's community.

As we reach out beyond our comfort zones and areas of influence we are guided by the words of Martin Luther King, Jr., "Justice at its best is love correcting everything that stands against love."

Engaged cosmology consists of a new vision of sacredness, grace, play, compassion, art, and joy – a radical inclusiveness that transforms domination into partnership and hierarchies into circles of collaboration, compassion, creativity, and reverence. New relationships of healing and interconnectedness will be born out of the awe and wonder revealed in the divine self-disclosure through the universe.

They will be activated by a theology of contemplation, liberation, and creation; healing and interconnectedness will be grounded in the biblical narratives that remind us that all life is holy, that every creature is loved and called to realize its full potential and contribute to a new humanity and a new creation through engagement and spirituality.

It is a great work for which all are needed. We join the great symphony of life, a masterpiece that honours the legacy and wisdom of those who came before. One of its many melodies brings to mind the words of Mahatma Gandhi, who said, "Peacemakers cannot afford to be 'helpless.' We must become the change we want to see in this world."

Mahatma Gandhi's work of nonviolence has been a beacon and guide for many prophets of civil rights and world peace in my lifetime. When I marched with Martin Luther King, Jr., in Detroit to support the civil rights movement, we were carrying the banner of Gandhi. When I joined the United Farm Workers in Toronto to protest the unjust sale of lettuce and grapes, I was aware that César Chávez was inspired by Gandhi.

When people gather in Fort Benning, Georgia, and join in a silent protest with members of the School of the Americas Watch to close this school of assassins, they follow not only their leader, Fr. Roy Bourgeois, MM, but also the great soul himself, Mahatma Gandhi. His approach is revealed in these words:

To conquer the subtle passions seems to me to be harder than the physical conquest of the world by force of arms.

With this in mind, we can awaken from the psychic numbness that paralyzes our culture and discover the new power surging through the universe and that is available in our spiritual traditions and operative in the biographies of engagement that articulate each of our lives. Pierre Teilhard de Chardin puts it well:

May you find the path which will lead you
to the highest and truest of yourself ...
Hope for perpetual discovery and trust life.
That's all.

A New Moment of Grace

Today well lived makes every yesterday a dream of happiness and every tomorrow a vision of hope.

—*From the Sanskrit*

The purpose of these pages is to create a synergy among the unfolding dynamics of the universe (the Great Story); the pre-existing commitment that resides in each of us as a result of our connection to our traditions, inspired by our scriptures; and the transformative work available to us in our culture (therapy, organizing, popular education, geo-justice, and engaged cosmology).

I believe we are searching for a movement, a human way to enter into the rhythms of the universe. We need to integrate existing networks that see personal and cultural events as empowered by and expressions of the universe itself. With such a vision we see a vast evolution of healing fueled by the energies of our greatest passions, a phenomenon much like the coming of spring, a sudden spontaneity where people "live what they sing about."

As we open ourselves to the opportunities of this moment, we see the future as a time in which the universe will act through us. It will be a time nourished by silence, energized by moral outrage, and characterized by a profound trust in life's unfolding. It will be a time to participate in whatever needs to be done.

It will be a time of a new vision, new language, new energy, and new actions.

It will be a time to embrace both beauty and brokenness as we discover a common language and take part in a common struggle to heal the separation between the biosphere (stars) and the street, the galaxies and the ghetto.

It will be a time to embrace our beauty and our wounds, to savour communion, and to celebrate the sequence of transformational events that have shaped our sense of the sacred.

It will be a time of unprecedented personal fulfillment and planetary peace.

It will be a time when each person will celebrate his or her life and offer their unique gifts to the universe, for each of us was shaped and formed in the same primordial furnace.

It will be a time to reinvent our lives, to become more fully aware of the universe, to delve into the wisdom contained in our traditions, and to transform culture through shared destiny, liberation, and profound fulfillment.

It will be a time when the stories of our lives will be congruent with the Great Story of the universe.

It will be a time for a new convergence of the mediating structures that emerge from work of cosmology, theology, and the social sciences (science, spirituality, and societal practice).

It will be a time when we wake from the dream of separateness and leap into this new moment in which we restructure society and restore the Earth.

It will be a time when experience is more important than ideas, and energy the most powerful experience of being alive.

It will be a time to break through the armor of the heart and open ourselves to the healing action of the Earth.

It will be a time to activate the imagination, a starting moment of hope when we will be astonished by our dreams and enchanted by a universe that can quench our thirst for wonder and liberate our hearts.

It will be a time for hesitation and hope, pain and possibility, wonder and surprise.

It will be a time of buoyancy as we navigate the turbulent waters of transition and change today, knowing that we are part of the changes we aspire to and work for.

> Fear and fulfillment
> permeate my soul
> as the culture turns.
> Renaissance becomes another word for hope.
> Presence and inclusion
> name our new day
> a time of engagement
> flowing from the heart of all.

The Path to Prolonged Engagement

Boldness has genius, power and magic in it.

Begin it now.

—Goethe

Sister Helen's Story

I first met Sister Helen Prejean, CSJ, at a conference on engaged cosmology in Los Gatos, California, in 2004. I had seen the movie *Dead Man Walking* and read her award-winning book. In person, she fulfills the biblical archetype of the reluctant prophet. Through correspondence with death-row inmates and accompanying them to execution, Sr. Helen has become an international spokesperson for the abolition of the death penalty. This gifted speaker is a woman of great faith, with a wonderful sense of humour and a dedication to justice that have placed her among the most prophetic voices of our day.

When Sister Helen heard the gospel phrase "they would be poor no more" her world turned and she embarked on a new path in her spiritual journey. She was gripped by the letters she received from death-penalty inmates. She could no longer condone the injustice of the death penalty.

She remembered the prophetic words of author William Faulkner, who wrote that "the only thing worth writing about is the conflict in the human heart."

Dead Man Walking by Sister Helen Prejean is in many ways a book for us all. In it we experience the challenge to appreciate the dignity of all individuals, no matter how dreadful their crimes. It is a story of awakening to the certainty that each of us is a miracle.

The Call to Participate

In our era, the road to holiness necessarily passes through the world of action.

—Dag Hammerskjold

Our reflection on engaged cosmology reminds us of the words of Mahatma Gandhi, who wrote, "Protest is my modus operandi." We unite our vision to the work of Teilhard de Chardin in his cry for "a new soul for a new world." Engagement is a way to heal, to overcome fear, to unite people around a common action. And so we take up a cosmological vision: we exercise our powers of the soul and engage in communication with both people and planet.

We question whether capitalism is compatible with mutuality and justice. We realize that we need to participate in the radical restructuring of society. We practice listening in order to unite our actions with the powers of the universe as they course through our veins.

As we gain access to this wisdom we become committed to challenging apathy and to opening the doors of engagement wherein reside not only the secrets of the human heart but the seeds of an authentic participatory democracy.

Our Place

In the mystical moist night air
I looked up in perfect silence
at the stars.

—*Walt Whitman*

As we ponder engaged cosmology we ask, why are we here? What are the fundamental roles we are called to fulfill? As we reflect on our planet, place, and path, and the despair and destruction that surround us, we feel challenged. We awaken both to our cosmological origins and to our capacity to live in the death of things. We begin to navigate the turbulent waters of this time, one of the darkest in human history. We learn that the language of the universe is a kind of music that is now becoming audible to us, resonant and complex.

We look for images to guide us on our journey; we reflect on the stars, the oceans, and cities. We recall that the stars are our ancestors: we are all made of stardust. It is through our wonder at the stars that the universe floods into us to heal our brokenness and to activate our capacity to marvel.

The oceans remind us that water can eventually dissolve anything. We begin to see that we have the capacity to dissolve barriers and heal the chasms that divide the human heart. We can then reach out, and as we do so, new experiences flood across our soul. We care deeply, obtain guidance for what needs to be done, and become a source of joy in our brokenhearted world as we strive to bring fulfillment to each person's life.

Cities become reminders that a challenge of engaged cosmology is to give birth to a new humanity coherent with the unfolding dynamics of the universe; each "new" human's consciousness and conscience will make it possible to embrace, give expression to, and participate in the energetic powers of the universe. We will become *fully* human.

Engaged cosmology includes a capacity to endure profound human pain. It also requires a process that liberates us from consumerism as we participate in what Brian Swimme describes as the "deep energy that wants to come forth and exult in the majesty of each moment." Our quest to become fully human will challenge us to explore and experience life intuitively. We are being invited into wisdom during our chaotic and turbulent times. The lyrical language of the poets speaks to this mystical dimension, to the experience of wisdom.

This approach encourages us to discover, as writer Margo Wheatley says, "patterns that will lead to meaningful experiences." Storytelling is the vehicle for transmitting wisdom. In telling stories the wild energy of creation remains active and present among us.

Engaged cosmology unfolds in the personal story; in reflection on our traditions, both cultural and religious; in naming our alignment with the universe; and in actions that increase our engagement through intimacy, justice-making, and networking.

We feel a growing conviction that because the cause is right, the cause will prevail. As Sister Helen Prejean tells us, "Things of justice are forged in the fire of our hearts." The soul-sizzled agenda of engaged cosmology will take us into future.

> I know
> that poverty must cease.
> I know this through the brokenness
> and conflict in my heart.
> I know
> that protest is my most prophetic act
> and that the world is longing
> for a new soul, a new healing moment.
> I know
> that when we awaken to our origins
> and become truly human
> we bring hope to the children
> and to the earth.
> I feel called today
> to bring the people together to break the bread
> and tell the story.
> I feel called today
> to be a mystic in action,
> aligned to the dynamics of the universe.
> I feel called today
> to give my gift,
> to listen to the heartbeat of the broken world;
> to heal the fragmentation of people and planet.
> I feel called today
> to celebrate the wonder of creation

and respond to sacredness and the
challenges of life.
I feel called today
to participate in the work of my time,
to fall in love,
to feel at home.
I feel called today
to be inflamed with enduring hope,
to be at one with the universe,
to be touched by God.
I feel called today
To compose a new paragraph for life.

Power and Celebration

The full power of ecology can only be felt in the realization
that the universe, the planet Earth, and all
living and non-living beings exist primarily for celebration.

—*Thomas Berry*

Engaged cosmology brings us into alignment with the unfolding dynamics of the universe. Our constant challenge is to conquer the energies that tend to distract us and overcome any tendencies that oppose our purpose and passion. We move forward with gratitude and hope, conscious of and committed to living within the guidance of the universe with its culminating energy, creativity, ability to act, depth, collaborative partnership, and capacity to render things sacred.

Something new breaks through as we awaken to the energy of the universe and the cosmic context of our lives. The insights and healing energies available from psychology, organization, politics, popular education, culture, and spirituality offer a fresh and dynamic integration and unfolding of the Great Story.

As we gain perspective on the challenges and accomplishments of the past, we anticipate a time when engaged cosmology will bring justice and peace to our endangered planet. As we contemplate our common origin as stardust, our awareness is flooded with a fresh realization that we are an expression of the wisdom that invites us to live more fully in mutually enhancing ways.

When this energy, generated from the awe and wonder of the universe, is aligned to the profound motivation prompted by faith traditions, we can look forward to a better world for all the children.

Healing Our Darkest Moment

We can never bring a healing to this continent until we are first blessed and first healed by this continent.

—Thomas Berry

Our world is replete with social systems that oppose their original purpose: one example is the media.

The media – radio, television, the Internet, and so on – play an important role in public life. We rely on them to provide us with accurate information, a necessary component for a democratic society. But the media can become entangled in presenting information to the public for the purpose of accomplishing a particular goal or agenda. Noam Chomsky, well-known linguist and scholar from the Massachusetts Institute of Technology, calls this approach "manufactured consent"; others have named this selective reporting as a state of "missing information."

The situation in the United States is an example of the difficulty and importance of the media. In the United States a small number of large corporations – about six – own all the major newspapers and networks. It is not difficult to see that the information disseminated is likely to have a bias toward big business.

The implications for politics and for the owners of the corporations are great. The public often receives distorted and even deliberately misleading "news" on such things as energy costs, the effects of big business on the environment, terrorist activities, supposed locations for weapons of mass destruction, and more.

Berkeley, California – where I currently live – is the home of KPFA, the country's original listener-sponsored radio station. This station does not take money from big corporations, only from individual donations. With this level of independence, it is free to tell "the real story."

National Public Radio (NPR) and the Public Broadcasting Service (PBS) stand somewhere between the corporate media and the free-speech media. There is constant controversy about the level of freedom they possess and the amount of corporate pressure that they endure in their function of "getting out the news."

Cable television and radio programs in the United States that feature spokespeople from Rush Limbaugh and Bill O'Reilly to Al Franken and Randy Rhodes illustrate the struggle to get the word out from a certain perspective.

In my experience, Canada's major network, CBC (Canadian Broadcasting Corporation), is a more reliable source of news than most big US stations. It offers facts rather than "interpretations" of the news.

Whatever your view, media that accurately present the news are irreplaceable in the healthy functioning of a participatory democracy. Our public life is in jeopardy as long as we accept programs that interpret the news rather than reporting it.

- The media distort the facts.
- Politics promotes war and oppresses people.
- Religions seek power rather than offer liberation.
- Corporations value products over people.
- Education teaches conformity to unjust systems.
- The penal system is a symbol of inequality.

In this darkest moment, we are called to transform

- unthinking consent into consciousness
- war into peace
- guilt into celebration
- sickness into health
- greed into generosity
- death into liberation and new life
- injustice into harmony, balance, and peace

Now is the time to become engaged, to be energized by the awe and wonder of the universe, to be activated by a greater trust in spiritual tradition, and to become participants in the defining moment of our day.

It is time to uplift our hearts, honour our ancestors, and speak back to power. We need to change this dark moment by igniting a beacon of hope. Courage can be contagious. As we learn to incarnate a new vision, tomorrow will be different.

I look in the human heart for the foundation stone of a new social impulse.

—*Mary Caroline Richards*

Our New Moment

A change in context can completely change our experience.

—*George Leonard*

We live in a world soaked in pain; soldiers and civilians die; the earth is laid waste with toxins; youth hover in despair. Yet, in the midst of this moment, the darkest in human history, a fresh renaissance is beginning to emerge.

We live in a new time; it is our time. It is the time of a metareligious movement when the God of the cosmos has come home to earth. It is a time when engaged wisdom will converge to resacralize the world.

It is our deep desire to contribute to the health of our planet, provide hope for the children and a channel of wisdom and creativity for all who are called to the great Work that lies ahead; the goal is to make possible a more mutually enhancing world.

They're a noble group of women and men with marinated souls, these people of the stars and the street.

People whose countenance shimmers with a radiance forged by years of generosity and service. People whose unforgotten wisdom is punctuated with moments of great joy and deep sorrow; their lives, deepened by courage and creativity, are forged in the embrace of inevitable burdens, yet remain radiant with gratitude and peace.

Reared in the cauldron of a nation they call home, their land is a place of many first communions where the "God of all things" becomes manifest in farms and fields, rivers and flowers, villages and cities. In this sacred gathering place, they learn more from rocks, water and trees and from engagement with the poor and most neglected than from the books of the masters.

This gathering place is a place to belong, a place for dreams of service and hope; dreams of answering an unexpected call to give their lives away, only to receive them back a hundredfold. Through countless acts of compassion and moments of grace, they discover in the joy of a child and the beauty of a sunrise and the cry of the poor encounters with their unknown God whose transparent presence shines through portals of joy, pain and surprise.

Narratives of service and the great galactic story have called them forth into a new chapter of life.

Each paragraph is forged by prophetic partnerships and the incarnation of a vision realized in unexpected ways; a new journey of courageous engagement born from acts of generosity and service as they become a "kingdom people."

It is a new testament prompted by a "sacred impulse," a holy longing, a deep desire to participate in a joyful, hope-filled journey that no one could have foreseen or planned.

These threshold people are positioned gracefully at the doorway of something entirely new. They feel called to incarnate a dream unimagined years ago. It is a new dream to discover the cosmic implications of their faith and a generous response to a call to befriend the earth.

This new dream, this mysterious excursion is evoked by the awesome beauty of the universe, a pre-existing commitment to a gospel of service and the noble narrative inscribed in each of their lives.

Today, these prophetic people stand positioned at a new defining moment, on the precipice of a meta-religious journey; they are announcing a new collective narrative from which beauty will shine forth to heal our brokenhearted world and unite the stars to the street.

The intoxication of advancing the kingdom in every domain of humanity.
—Teilhard de Chardin

You were made for these times.
—Clarissa Pinkola Estes

Acclamations

After the violence
Wisdom speaks.
Find the fire.
Attend to divine nudges.
Venture to the threshold.
Let stars announce your name.
Proclaim a hymn to the universe.
Sing a compassionate embrace.

Epilogue

Looking Back through the Lens
of Engaged Cosmology

For every poet there is always morning in the world.

–Derek Walcott

Engaged wisdom is a manifestation of soul, embraced by divine creative energy that flows through each person, permeates the cosmos and summons us to life; a life of seeking, ceremony and depth, that is a foundation for all peoples, all energy and the earth; a life that cries out in silent hunger for what lies hidden within.

Engaged wisdom is a celebration of awe and wonder that nourishes courage and creativity, to navigate the cultural waters of uncertainty and depth.

Engaged wisdom is present in stories retrieved through thought, memory, engagement. It reminds us of origins and of a tomorrow we hope will happen now.

Engaged wisdom gives voice to the silent cry, the unspoken hunger that gains access to the as yet inaudible voice that cries out from the brokenhearted world and from the heart of the universe itself.

Engaged wisdom enhances our capacity for receptivity; we hear the silent hunger of an Iraqi child and the pain of a meadow singed with acid rain, the result of global warming.

Engaged wisdom invites us to view the earth community as a wisdom circle; we listen keenly to the promptings of our heart manifest emanating from the heart of the cosmos.

Engaged wisdom arouses us by the "eros of unjustice" and calls us forth to co-create the conditions by which beauty can shine forth; we experience a sacramental consciousness and view every sight, sound, smell, joy, sorrow and touch as an experience of divinity and a source of primary revelation.

Engaged wisdom celebrates an integral ecology and an eco-mysticism; we realize with Rilke that "words are the last resort for what lies deep within"; we savour the divine creative energy that permeates existence and summons us to life.

Through engaged wisdom we hear a lyrical language expressing the ecological mystery at the centre of existence. As we stand at the shore and listen to the universe, we realize that God is a poet and the universe is God's manuscript.

Through engaged wisdom and the practice of integral ecology we become energized to heal our brokenhearted world and metastasized culture. Martin Luther King, Jr., wrote, "the arc of the universe is long and it bends toward justice"; our call is to become both a poet and politician; to be transparent, receptive, open, poetic, political, silent, restless, and engaged.

Through the practice of engaged wisdom we embrace the paradox of existence and connect the apparent opposites of intimacy and contemplation, terror and peace, life and death, beginnings and endings. We respond to the silent cry and unspoken hunger for oneness and relationship.

From the shores of the new millennium we sail onto the turbulent waters of society. Through engaged wisdom we become hospice workers for structures that need to die with dignity and midwives for a new era about to be born.

The Rest of the Way

Learn to listen as subjects speak for themselves.

—*Danny Martin*

Engaged cosmology creates the context and the conditions from which beauty can shine forth.

We are called to contribute to the future; to join our energy with those overarching movements of the universe whose dynamics urge us forward; to realize a radical reinvention of society and self. With a renewed sensitivity we will align our creativity with the whole cosmic process, carried forth by a transcendent sense of hope for a world at the threshold of peace.

With a greater sense of trust, we cast our lot, convinced that those powers of the universe that brought us here will take us forward.

Making Sense of Mystery!

Making sense of mystery
touches the divine madness
that reveals the wildness
and erotic energy
of an untamed God.

As we penetrate the illusion of separateness,
trust the promptings that emerge from
the deep mystery in our midst, and
reinvent the practice of strategic action
for this new time.

We stand today at a precipice, that
holds the promise of an "integral life."

We embrace ambiguity and let go of
forms and stories that defined a
previous life.

We explore the meaning of mystery and
connect our quest with the originating
energy of the universe.

We swim into an ocean of mystery, carried
forward by the fetal waters of the cosmos.

Here beyond conscious thought we touch
the Divine whose presence is proclaimed
in image, sight and sound.

Within this seamless garment
Engaged Cosmology appears and
beauty shines forth.

I Hope to be Remembered

Each of us is a novice in the monastery of the cosmos, embracing the vow or relationship, our hearts broken open by the beauty and pain of our planetary home.

I hope to be remembered …
As someone who lived on Earth
Expressed compassion to creation
Listened deeply with my heart
And experienced communion
With those most neglected and abused.
As someone whose acts of creativity
Lived on after my time,
Projects and people enveloped in the beauty of creation
Communing with the recesses of my soul.
As someone who embraced fully
The beauty and brokenness of life
The hopes, joys and sorrows of the moment
And worked to make them gestures of generosity
To heal a brokenhearted world.
And to say when it is finished
    I am grateful
    I have done my best
    I have no regrets

I am convinced that the universe is under the control of a loving purpose and that in the struggle for righteousness man (sic) has cosmic companionship.

—*Martin Luther King Jr.*

After-words

A Canticle to the Stars and the Street

Newness erupts from the abyss
Narratives unfold
We locate ourselves in the cosmic dance
From which The Great Story is told.

In transparent vulnerability
We listen with our heart
To the messengers of God
And are moved to heal a broken world.

A new paragraph is written
Inscribed in beauty and in pain
As we take up the privileged task of love
And see the great Work of Justice as our
        deepest prayer.

Moved by an emerging awareness
That our developmental task
Is to build the kingdom (of God) here on Earth
We begin.

We navigate life's uncertain waters
Look with hope toward tomorrow
And cross the threshold of engagement
Through a tapestry of beauty and love
To nurture a world of justice.

As exegetes of the new creation
To resacralize the world
We discover within the depths of every
    mountain and snowflake
A message from our God.

From the fireball of our origins
We discover within opaqueness and pain
A new-found ability to act
And heal a brokenhearted world.

We entertain a vision of home for the children
And are enveloped in a fresh desire
To quench the thirst for oneness
With creation and our God.

With fresh appreciation for beauty
We resacralize the world
And discover in each expression of creation
The language of the Earth.

With new-found literacy and realization
We enter the promised land of home
Leave behind pathos and pathology
And embark upon a landscape of new hope.

Breaking out of structures of conformity
And enveloped in a divine embrace
We wander forth into new beginnings
And see each as an expression of the
    reign of God.

We fashion forth
Fresh motifs of transformation
And learn again the language of the soul
To make audible a chorus of creation
Where every voice is heard.

We traverse the doorway of engagement
To enact a paschal mystery story for our time
Summoned by the voices of creation
To do our transformation task.

A planetary Pentecost
Manifest in our midst
Is strengthened by the bonds
        of a new creation
Clothed in a garment of peace.

Enveloped by a cosmic crucifixion
We are aroused to make our Easter with the Earth.
Energized by this fresh fluorescence
We take up our epic of engagement task
To celebrate the paschal mystery story
        in our time.

Our task is one of generosity, sacrifice and self-transcendence
A task to support those most endangered and abused
A task to encourage community and relatedness
A task to support the self-healing properties
        of creation and soul
A task of responding to the felt-sense of a "sacred impulse"
        whose originating energies give birth to the
        universe and self
A task to nurture harmony, balance and peace
A task to create a new synthesis of consciousness
        and conscience in alignment between cultural
        work and the dynamics of the universe
A task to embrace new beginnings, Gethsemane moments,
        and the inevitable outpouring of new life
A task to perceive each of our lives as a story,
        a paragraph in the new story, a context from
        which to create actions to transform the world
A task of deep listening, understood as an echo
        from the heart of the universe that evokes
        a fabric of meaning and moments of mutuality

A task to participate in projects and processes
      that nurture and celebrate interdependence,
      the desire for freedom and reverence for a
      resacralized earth
A task to support and protect the little ones and
      awaken the imagination of youth as a portal
      and promise of the future
A task to dissolve any sense of separation, exile,
      alienation or loneliness and work to make
      possible the experience of belonging
A task to make possible opportunities for
      creativity and the celebration of life.

Eros invites me
To the threshold of desire
Where the quest for justice
Becomes another word for God.

Embraced by the universe
I strive to heal the fragmentation
That fractures my psyche
To heal the hunger for oneness in my soul.

The story of engagement unfolds
New alternatives emerge
In our aspirations
We find hope for an unfolding future.

We awaken to a new era
To dawn and dusk
Beauty and brokenness
And remember that we are genetically
      coded for new hope.

Bathed in the beauty of each day
We awaken to a new defining moment
Honour Teilhard and Thomas
And take up the change of their vision.

Engaged wisdom for a brokenhearted world
Spontaneously springs forth
In a time of prophecy over profits
And wisdom over words.

The beauty of creation
Flowers forth
Transformation happens
Mutuality takes place.

Symphonic voices of creation
        present their clarion call
Exaltations in the mountains, rivers,
        meadows, birds and brooks
Awaken each of us to new depths of freedom
        and fulfillment.

Transformative litanies burst forth
Freedom rings out as once again
We bring back to awareness
What we most deeply know.

The language of the universe
Pulsates in our soul
We celebrate the compassion of creation
And listen to narratives in barrios,
        ghettos, circles of wisdom
And communities of hope.

Called forth by wisdom crisis
We edge unknowingly
To the precipice of our era and our time
Summoned by the lyrics of creation
And the sacred impulse of our lives
We rediscover new-found freedom which
        lives on among us to illuminate our day
        toward "shared destiny, deep liberation
        and profound fulfillment."

Awash in this sacred circle
Nurtured by kinship and creation and the
Depths of self-discovery
I set about to heal our broken world.

We take up the task of healing
Energized by connections to our wound
We proclaim a canticle of engagement
And take up the planetary task to renew
            the face of the earth.

Wisdom rustles through the wind
Empowered by the sun
We rise to celebrate the freedom of a new day.

Free of all blocks
Free of all structure
Embraced by the freedom
Of a liberated God.

Poets are most profoundly in communion with other modes of under-
standing.

                                          —*Thomas Berry*

Appendix: Action Autobiography

- What is your earliest recollection of an action through which you tried to bring change?
- How was this action a statement of hope and courage and confrontation with resignation and inertia?
- How did your action result in increased solidarity with others?
- Did this action increase your belief in people as a source of action on behalf of freedom, equality and peace?
- What people bring hope, promote freedom and model courage and compassion?
- How are you engaged with the forces of oppression and the symbols and sources of limitations in your life?
- What has been your most prophetic effort on behalf of Earth?
- What universal principles do you believe in and how do they serve to guide your work?
- In what ways have you worked toward unity between your awareness of the new cosmology and your actions for Earth?
- What have you learned about yourself and Earth through your efforts?
- What continues to hold you back?
- What have you seen, felt, or done to increase your efforts? What do you intend to do?
- How have your efforts toward freedom deepened your experience of the divine?
- What do you want to create on behalf of Earth in the next phase of your journey?

Preamble: The Earth Charter

We stand at a critical moment in Earth's history, a time when humanity must choose its future. As the world becomes increasingly interdependent and fragile, the future at once holds great peril and great promise. To move forward we must recognize that in the midst of a magnificent diversity of cultures and life forms we are one human family and one Earth community with a common destiny. We must join together to bring forth a sustainable global society founded on respect for nature, universal human rights, economic justice, and a culture of peace. Towards this end, it is imperative that we, the peoples of Earth, declare our responsibility to one another, to the greater community of life, and to future generations.

Earth, Our Home Humanity, is part of a vast evolving universe. Earth, our home, is alive with a unique community of life. The forces of nature make existence a demanding and uncertain adventure, but Earth has provided the conditions essential to life's evolution. The resilience of the community of life and the well-being of humanity depend upon preserving a healthy biosphere with all its ecological systems, a rich variety of plants and animals, fertile soils, pure waters, and clean air. The global environment with its finite resources is a common concern of all peoples. The protection of Earth's vitality, diversity, and beauty is a sacred trust.

The Global Situation. The dominant patterns of production and consumption are causing environmental devastation, the depletion of resources, and a massive extinction of species. Communities are being undermined. The benefits of development are not shared equitably and the gap between rich and poor is widening. Injustice, poverty, ignorance, and violent conflict are widespread and the cause of great suffering. An unprecedented rise in human population has overburdened ecological and social systems. The foundations of global security are threatened. These trends are perilous – but not inevitable.

The Challenges Ahead. The choice is ours: form a global partnership to care for Earth and one another or risk the destruction of ourselves and the diversity of life. Fundamental changes are needed in our values, institutions, and ways of living. We must realize that when basic needs have been met, human development is primarily about being more, not having more. We have the knowledge and technology to provide for all and to reduce our impacts on the environment. The emergence of a global civil society is creating new opportunities to build a democratic and humane world. Our environmental, economic, political, social, and spiritual challenges are interconnected, and together we can forge inclusive solutions.

Universal Responsibility. To realize these aspirations, we must decide to live with a sense of universal responsibility, identifying ourselves with the whole Earth community as well as our local communities. We are at once citizens of different nations and of one world in which the local and global are linked. Everyone shares responsibility for the present and future well-being of the human family and the larger living world. The spirit of human solidarity and kinship with all life is strengthened when we live with reverence for the mystery of being, gratitude for the gift of life, and humility regarding the human place in nature.

We urgently need a shared vision of basic values to provide an ethical foundation for the emerging world community.

Ecozoic Council

(www.ecozoiccouncil.net)

Ecozoic points to a new awareness in human consciousness which recognizes the Universe as revelatory of the Divine.

A context for cosmic connections to provide information, support and the possibility of common action for people and projects whose conscious self-awareness has inspired them to participate in mutually enhancing relationships to celebrate and protect our sacred planetary home.

Contact information for Jim Conlon:
Web site: www.jimconlon.net
e-mail: jacstory@aol.com

About the Author

Jim Conlon, Ph.D., was born in Ontario, Canada, in the Great Lakes bioregion. He is chairperson of the Sophia Center in Culture and Spirituality at Holy Names University in Oakland, California, and the author of *From the Stars to the Street*; *At the Edge of Our Longing*; *The Sacred Impulse*; *Ponderings from the Precipice*; *Lyrics for Re-Creation*; *Earth Story, Sacred Story*; and *Geo-Justice*.

Praise for *From the Stars to the Street*

"True contemplatives are not dreamers. Their eyes hold a vision, while their hands translate that vision into action. This is what Jim Conlon does. In *From the Stars to the Street,* he invites us to share in the work of healing our brokenhearted world. Many will find strength for this task through the engaged wisdom of today's prophets, brought together from many sources in these pages."—*Brother David Steindl-Rast, OSB, www.gratefulness.org*

"In this signature work, Jim Conlon shows us how to bring the cosmological vision of Thomas Berry into a comprehensive program for transforming our world from the industrial growth paradigm to a mutually enhancing human/earth relations."—*Brian Swimme*

"Jim Conlon's *From the Stars to the Street* takes us not only on his personal life's path but expands that to the journey of the poor, the disenfranchised, the forgotten, the ignored, the mistreated, and the abused Earth itself. Bringing to bear the experiences of his childhood in a village in Canada, his seminary training, his years of community organizing, his preparation for ministry, his awakening to the Great Story and geo-justice, and the mentors who guided his way – Freire, Alinsky, Berry, and others – Jim speaks out loud and clear for the voiceless, both human and nonhuman, who are ground up and thrown away by our frenetic, over-consuming culture. Seldom has an author made it clearer that his personal life story, our stories, and the Earth's story are individual threads of the Kingdom of God. *From the Stars to the Street* is an invigorating tonic for those who may have become tired in the struggle for justice and a motivation to action for those who are just beginning to see their role in the Great Story."—*Sister Helen Prejean*

"This is the book that we have been waiting for. Jim Conlon offers a cosmology that stitches personal narrative, experiential parables, and egalitarian rhetoric together. *From the Stars to the Street* reminds us that we are here to pursue those activities that will render humankind and the planet whole."—*Barbara Holmes, PhD*

"Jim Conlon's insights into his personal journey, as well as the collective quest of a generation, illuminate paths by which we can recognize our lives and actions as constituting an 'intimate moral presence' to and for the Earth Community and the unfolding cosmos. Both visionary and pragmatic, *From the Stars to the Street* is an urgently needed book."—*Charlene Spretnak, Author of* Missing Mary

"Life is a tapestry of wisdom continually evolving, and even when it unravels, it remains the handiwork of the Divine proclaiming all is one. That is Jim Conlon's credo. As one who has walked the streets, wrestled with reality, and still cherishes the stars, he writes with integrity, giving testimony to how we can come home to our cosmic and planetary roots – and why it is essential to do so."—*Miriam Therese Winter*